The Paradise of the Soul

The Paradise of the Soul

Forty-Two Virtues to Reach Heaven

SAINT ALBERT THE GREAT

Translated by
Fr. Robert Nixon, OSB

TAN Books
Gastonia, North Carolina

Translated by Fr. Robert Nixon, OSB

Cover design by Jordan Avery

Cover image: The Assumption of the Virgin Mary, 1642, by Guido Reni (1575-1642). Alte Pinakothek, Munich, Germany. Tarker / Bridgeman images.

Interior image: Saint Albertus Magnus, engraving 1851 / Bridgeman images.

ISBN: 978-1-5051-2809-3
Kindle ISBN: 978-1-5051-2810-9
ePUB ISBN: 978-1-5051-2809-3

Published in the United States by
TAN Books
PO Box 269
Gastonia, NC 28053
www.TANBooks.com

Printed in India

"*Albert the Great was a man who knew all that could be known, who lacked knowledge of no field of learning.*"

—Pope Pius II

"*Albert the Great is such a saint as our own age, which seeks peace and promises marvels to itself from the sciences, is able to gaze upon with intent eyes, and to derive great benefit from his example.*"

—Pope Pius XI

Contents

Contents

TRANSLATOR'S NOTE

The flourishing of virtues is the surest and most reliable sign of a sound spiritual life. Hence there is no more effective way of attaining spiritual progress than by the conscious cultivation of the virtues. It is this goal—the cultivation of the virtues—which is the theme of this fascinating work.

The word "virtue" is a translation of the Latin term *virtus*, which is etymologically related to both the words *vis* (strength) and *vir* (man). Each of the virtues is therefore something which reflects and promotes "strength of character." These virtues (or strengths) stand in opposition to the vices (in Latin *vitia*, meaning "weaknesses"). By cultivating the virtues, an individual becomes stronger, more fulfilled, closer to God, more authentically human, and ultimately happier. This happiness can be experienced during the present life, but it reaches its supreme perfection only in the kingdom of heaven. The virtues serve as reliable guideposts to the soul as it makes its way to this realm of eternal bliss, where, freed from all sinfulness and sorrow, it will enjoy forever the glorious presence of God Himself.

The author of this work, Saint Albert the Great (c.1200–80), was eminently qualified to address the topic of the virtues. He was a Dominican friar who served as archbishop of the German city of Regensburg. Reputed to be the most learned man of his time, one of Albert's greatest distinctions is that he was the principal teacher of Saint Thomas Aquinas, the Angelic Doctor. Albert's corpus of writings is vast and all-encompassing. A true polymath, he was an expert not only on theology, philosophy, and Sacred Scripture but also on chemistry, medicine, botany, zoology, and astronomy. It is very appropriate, therefore, that he is known by the appellation of *Doctor Universalis*, or Universal Doctor.

His treatise on the virtues, entitled *Paradisus Animae* ("The Paradise of the Soul") reflects his systematic and analytical approach. His comprehensive knowledge of Church doctrine, Scripture, and the writings of the Church Fathers is supported by his own remarkably perceptive and subtle insights into human behavior and psychology.

In preparing this translation, an effort has been made to convey Albert's intended meanings as faithfully as possible, but in a way that will be readily understood by contemporary readers. Footnotes have been added to elucidate passages and points which may not be entirely clear. Text in square brackets [ ] indicates insertions by the translator to complete or clarify the sense of the original.

One of Albert's most striking ideas, articulated in his prologue, is that each of the virtues stands in a direct relation to a particular vice. Thus if any virtue is taken to an extreme, it ceases to be a virtue and becomes a vice. For example, if a sense of justice is carried too far, it may become severity or harshness. On the other hand, if mercy or tolerance is taken too far, it may degenerate into permissiveness or laxity. For Albert, like Aristotle, true virtue is to be found in the golden mean, between two possible and antithetical extremes.

In this magisterial treatise, Albert devotes a chapter to forty-two different virtues. Each of these is followed by a short prayer to God for the acquirement of that particular virtue, taken from (or based upon) those in the 1595 Prague edition of the work.

As the teacher of Thomas Aquinas, Albert the Great is certainly a mentor of proven capacity and effectiveness. In reading and reflecting upon his wonderful and profound thoughts in this present volume, the modern reader is sure to make progress in those virtues which lead both to tranquility and confidence in this present life and to eternal happiness in the next.

Sancte Alberte Magne, duc nos, doce nos, et ora pro nobis!
Saint Albert the Great, lead us, teach us, and pray for us!

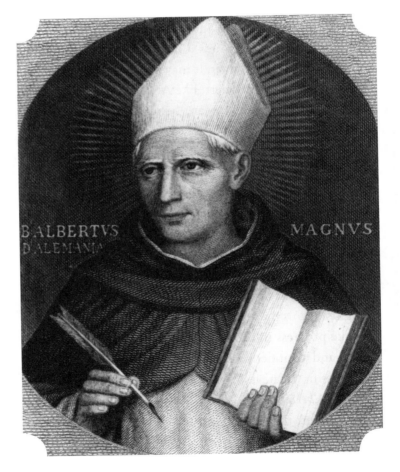

B.ALBERTVS
D.ALEMANIA

MAGNVS

THE LIFE OF SAINT ALBERT THE GREAT

From the *Proprium Festorum Diœcesis Spirensis*, 1860.

Albert was born in the venerable town of Lauingen in the province of Swabia [in Germany] to parents of noble and knightly rank. From his early youth, he entered upon the way of the Lord. While still an adolescent, he was sent to Padua, that noble city in Lombardy, where he acquired a firm basis for both the virtues and learning.

One day, he entered the basilica in that city and was meditating ardently upon how he could pursue a life of greater sanctity and devotion. As he deliberated thus, he commended himself in prayer to the Virgin Mary. And, behold, the Mother of all graces suddenly appeared to him! She urged him to enter the Order of Preachers, which at the time was still a newly founded institution, yet one which was flourishing in a marvelous fashion. The Queen of Heaven also confided to him that if he did so, he would be enriched with all the treasures of celestial wisdom and would illuminate the entire Christian world. Albert took prompt and enthusiastic heed of the Mother of God's counsels and immediately sought admission to the Order of Preachers. He very soon received the habit of the Dominicans from Blessed Jordan of Saxony, the superior general of the order at the time.

Having accepted the habit of pious conversion, he devoted himself totally to sacred studies. And such was his industry and intelligence that he soon came to be considered a font of all knowledge, overflowing with true wisdom. Such was his brilliance that he shed glorious luster upon many of the most noble academic seats in Germany—namely Cologne, Hildesheim, Strasburg, Freiburg, and Regensburg. His most penetrating interpretations of the holy writings, the fame of his sanctity and wondrous learning, and the immaculate example of his life soon became known throughout the entire Catholic world. By defeating heresies and refuting errors, he saved countless souls from damnation.

Hence it was that the supreme pontiff, Pope Alexandar IV, with the support of the whole college of cardinals, chose Albert as bishop of the church of Regensburg. Albert himself was reluctant to accept this high dignity on account of his humility and his devotion to austerity of life, but in obedience to the pope, he agreed. He was received as bishop with the greatest joy and jubilation from all the clergy and people of the city.

Having been consecrated as bishop and while occupying the episcopal throne, he never ceased to remember the humility, poverty, and disciplines of religious life to which he had committed himself in his vows. The episcopal residence, known as Thumstauf, located about one mile away from the city, became a place of peaceful refuge for his devotions and meditations. At Thumstauf, he wrote his great commentary on the Gospel of Luke.

After he had served as bishop for a few short years in a most praiseworthy manner, he sought to return to his own Dominican Order and to the academic life. Thus, in the year 1262, with the consent of Pope Urban IV, he handed over his episcopal responsibilities to Leo, a most creditable man. Albert himself, greatly refreshed in his spirit, returned to Cologne and resumed his academic post.

The remarkable sanctity and wisdom which Albert possessed is shown by the fact that the Angelic Doctor, Saint Thomas Aquinas, was one of his students.

It was the reasoning and eloquence of Albert that persuaded the Holy See to grant confirmation to the election of Rudolf of Hapsburg as the Holy Roman emperor. By virtue of his diplomacy and prudence as a negotiator, he was able to restore peace between Wilhelm, the count of Jülichgau, and the city of Cologne.

At last, having reached his eightieth year and full of days, and yearning for the promised land of the eternal kingdom,

Albert passed over to the Lord on November 15, 1280, in the seventh year of the reign of the emperor Rudolf. The body of the saint was laid to rest in the Church of the Holy Cross, which he himself had erected, in the presence of Siegfried, the archbishop of Cologne. At the request of Albert IV, the bishop of Regensburg, Pope Gregory XV established the annual observance of a feast in veneration of Albert the Great.

SAINT ALBERT'S PROLOGUE

There are certain vices which frequently assume the appearance of the virtues. And thus, though they are actually vices, they are wrongly believed to be virtues. For example, severity can seem like justice. Cynicism can seem like maturity. Loquaciousness is sometimes believed to be affability. A dissolute person can be seen to be filled with a spirit of joy.

Often sloth or self-indulgent melancholy can seem to be commendable gravity and seriousness. A lack of enthusiasm or inertia can seem like discretion. Excessive and vain fastidiousness can seem like commendable cleanliness. Gluttony may be mistaken for a healthy appetite. Wastefulness can look like generosity, and miserliness is sometimes perceived as wise frugality.

> Stubbornness may be seen as constancy;
> dishonesty may be seen as discretion;
> hypocrisy may be seen as sanctity;

1

carelessness and negligence may be seen as mild
   tolerance;
curiosity may be seen as circumspection;
vainglory may be seen as straightforward
   self-esteem;
presumption may be seen as optimism;
carnal affection may be seen as charity;
arrogant and tyrannical correction of others may be
   seen as love of justice;
timidity may be seen as mercy, kindness or
   peacefulness;
and so on, for many others.

These vices that look like virtues may be compared to counterfeit coins, which are very easily mistaken for the genuine currency of true virtue. But, while the "counterfeit coins" of these false virtues may readily deceive human beings, they are not able to purchase one's entrance into the kingdom of heaven!

Certain virtues are natural, arising spontaneously from our human nature. Thus humility, kindness, modesty, generosity, mercy, and patience are often born in our hearts without any training or effort. But these virtues, which are simply part of the nature of some people, are not sufficient in themselves to merit an eternal reward or the kingdom of God, since they do not take any effort or resolution to acquire. Rather, our virtues must be developed beyond our purely natural characteristics, as a result of effort, intention, goodwill, and training, in order to possess true merit in the sight of God.

Now, just as certain vices are sometimes mistakenly judged to be virtues, so certain virtues can often appear to be vices. For example, justice may seem like severity, or maturity may seem like cynicism. Careful providence may seem like stinginess, and constancy may seem like stubbornness. Indeed, all the examples given earlier may be reversed in this way.

Occasionally, genuinely humble people are even accused of acting humbly as a result of some underlying vainglory. Sometimes, when people are genuinely holy, they may be seen as hypocrites by others. And sometimes something which is done out of the purest charity may even be attributed to motives of hatred or vindictiveness.

Thus it is very difficult to discern accurately between the vices and the virtues. Furthermore, each virtue has different degrees and grades. The first step in each virtue always comes solely through a gift or grace from God. But each of these virtues infused into us by divine grace ought to be increased and developed by human effort. For it is only when the virtues have reached their perfection in us that we have arrived at the destination and goal which God intends for us.

We shall start our discussion of the virtues with love, the mother and adornment of all the other virtues.

LOVE

LOVE OF GOD

The love of God is perfect when the soul offers itself up to God ardently and completely, and seeks from God no transitory comfort, nor even any eternal reward in return. Rather, it loves God not for the sake of any recompense but solely on account of the goodness, sanctity, and perfection which is inherent in His divine nature. Indeed, the sensitive and holy soul is repelled by the very idea of loving God with any ulterior or mercenary motive, such as gaining some comfort or reward from Him.

For God loves us freely, and pours out His strength into our souls. He does not do this because He hopes to receive anything useful from us in return, but rather He desires only to share with us His own natural and infinite beatitude and blessedness. The person who loves God solely because of His goodness and blessedness, and from an earnest desire to participate in the same goodness and blessedness of God, may be said to love God perfectly.

True knowledge of God leads the soul to this perfect love. For in the essence of God, all that is worthy of love is to be found—nobility, sanctity, power, wisdom, kindness, beauty, providence, and so forth. Similarly, the love that God has for us is eternal and boundless, not passing and contingent. A true perception of the nature of God's love for us leads the soul to love God with a similar type of love.

In the Gospel of John, God gives us a reliable indication of true love for Him, when He says, "The one who loves me keeps my commandments."[1] Saint Augustine echoes the same thought when he says, "We truly love God only to the extent that we keep His commandments." Keeping vows that we have made in the presence of God may also be seen as keeping His commandments, since we are bound to obey such vows just as much as we are bound to obey the divine mandates.

Saint Gregory the Great admonishes us, "Reflect carefully upon yourselves! And enquire diligently if you truly love God above all else." And no one should believe themselves to love God above all else if their actions do not bear this out. For perfect love of the Creator requires the testimony not only of our words, or even of our hearts, but also of our whole lives. The love of God is never inactive; rather, it

[1] John 14:21.

always manifests itself in works. If love does not show itself in action, then it is not really love at all.

Our obedience to the commandments and our performance of good works should be entirely pure in their intention. They should be done neither out of fear of punishment nor desire for any reward, as Saint Augustine testified. The one who loves God perfectly fulfills His commandments not out of dread of punishment or ambition to attain rewards. But rather, he obeys God because he knows that everything which God commands is perfect and good.

There are two reliable signs of true love towards God. The first is when a person rejoices in God in all things, regardless of what happens (whether it seems good or bad), in all times and all places. A purely natural love of God [that is, loving God when He sends obvious blessings and good fortune] does not merit any praise or credit from God. For such a love is motivated by self-interest and seeks only what is good for itself. Rather, it is only the free love of God—that is, loving God for His own goodness and not for the sake of oneself—which is truly perfect.

The second sign of true love for God is when a person is genuinely saddened by all things that displease God, whenever and wherever they occur, regardless of whether or not they affect him personally.

LOVE OF ONE'S NEIGHBOR

True love of one's neighbor is to love him just as one loves oneself, regardless of whether he is a friend or a foe. As Saint Augustine says, "To love one's neighbor as oneself means to love him in God and for the sake of God."

By loving him thus in God and for God, one does indeed truly love one's neighbor as oneself. For each person naturally desires good for himself and seeks to avoid what is bad. This same desire should extend equally to others. Each human being naturally seeks the well-being of his body and soul, and each human being naturally flees from whatever is detrimental to such well-being. And in the same manner should each Christian desire the good of others and seek to avert whatever is harmful to their well-being. This applies equally whether they are a friend or an enemy.

And while the commandment to love our neighbor requires us to love them in the same *way* that we love ourselves (that is, by desiring the good for them and wishing to minimize whatever is bad), it does not, of course, demand that we feel the same degree of ardor or expend the same level of effort in this love.

The natural affection for one's friends does not amount to true charity. For, as the Gospel declares, "even the pagans love those who love them." But to love one's enemies is *always* true charity, since it is never the result of natural affections. To love those who love you is merely the work of nature, but to confer benefits on those who do *not* love you is a characteristic of perfect charity. Although, as has been noted, the commandment does not require us to love others with equal fervor or effort, nevertheless to love one's enemies and one's friends with equal intensity is a wonderful sign of perfect charity. This means exhibiting equal kindness to those who correct and reprimand as to those who praise and bless, and to show equal kindness to those who vituperate you as to those who applaud you.

For, as Saint John Chrysostom testifies, there is nothing which makes us so like God as treating those who are hostile to us and those who love us with equal kindness. Indeed, we certainly attain to greater grace and glory through sustaining persecution than we do by enjoying favor, provided we respond with charity and patience. Thus it was that the enemies of the martyrs contributed more to their glory than did their friends.

Nature itself ought to lead us to love our neighbor, for all creatures love those who are similar to themselves. Thus it is that all human beings owe each other a debt of love—for each of them similarly bears the image of God, as Scripture testifies.

Proof of true charity is to feel compassion for your enemies, and not only your friends, in times of adversity. It is also to feel truly happy for the sake of your enemy whenever prosperity befalls him. This is indeed a very rare thing in this world!

In contrast, there are other feelings which are evidence of true hatred, which is the antithesis of love. This includes being struck with sadness and dejection whenever we see a certain person's face, or being filled with bitterness and gall whenever we hear him speak or even hear his name mentioned. To seek to impede whatever might bring him prosperity is similarly a sign of hatred, as is the disparagement and detraction of whatever good qualities he may possess.

Our Lord Jesus Christ exhibited none of these things in His treatment of Judas, even though He knew that he was to betray Him. On the contrary, He broke bread for him at the Last Supper, treating him in exactly the same manner as He treated all the other apostles. Even at the time of His betrayal, Christ did not deny a kiss to the traitor Judas but greeted Him with all kindness and civility. As Saint Jerome comments, Christ felt more sadness for the tragedy and shame that was about to strike Judas than He did for His own impending death.

For many people, it seems enough that they hope for their enemies' eternal salvation without wishing for their good or happiness in this present world. But eternal salvation is something which they are neither able to give them nor to take away from them! They seem to wish to forget that when Christ laid down His life for His enemies, He bound us not only to love our enemies but also to be ready to make a sacrifice of our own resources and our own selves for the well-being of our brothers and sisters in times of need. This obligation applies above all to those charged with the pastoral care of souls.

Two things particularly help to nourish the virtue of love. Our love for God is nourished by carefully observing His commandments, as is stated in the verse: "If you keep My commandments, you will remain in My love, just as I keep the commandments of My Father, and remain in His love."[2] Our love for our neighbor is nourished by cultivating feelings of compassion towards him and sincere sympathy for his sufferings, as is stated in Ecclesiasticus: "Do not withhold your compassion from those who weep, and walk with those who mourn. Do not disdain to visit the sick. Through these actions, you shall be confirmed in your love."[3]

Prayer to God for Love

O eternal Love and infinite goodness, in whom all the causes for all holy loves are contained! Through that immense and incomprehensible love by which You have bound Yourself to me, I beseech You to pour forth into my soul something of that same love. By means of this love, I pray that I may seek nothing of my own comfort or convenience but rather

---

[2]   John 15:10.
[3]   Ecclesiasticus 7:38–39.

love all other things, even myself, in absolute purity and for Your sake alone.

O Lord, make me imitate Your superabundant and inestimable charity, which infinitely exceeds the brilliance of the sun! For just as the sun sends it rays freely without expecting to gain any benefit for itself in return, even so does Your love radiate forth to all the universe. Lord, make me obey Your most just and holy commandments with all reverence and solicitude; for to do so is a clear indication of Your grace and of love of You. May my soul rejoice and give thanks to You for all things which are pleasing to You, O Lord, and be saddened only by those things which offend You.

May I love my neighbor in You and for Your sake. Teach me to seek those things which I should desire, and to flee from those things which I should avoid. May I wish good things to those who wish bad things for me, for to do so is pleasing to You. May I overcome my enemies by no other means than kindness and goodwill!

May I accept adversity with patience, for it is often the source of greater spiritual benefits than prosperity. May I suffer with those who suffer, and rejoice with those who rejoice. For each of my neighbors has the same human nature as I do, and each bears Your image and likeness. For You confer immortal glory upon those who imitate Your divine love, and thus show themselves to be true sons and daughters of You, our heavenly Father. Amen.

2

HUMILITY

Humility is truly perfect when it does not seek to be recognized for what it is. Indeed, true humility fears being clearly perceived, and thus earning the praise and approval of others. It prefers not to receive any praise or approval from human beings, because it knows that glory and honor are due to God alone. And true humility takes no delight in any glory and praise, unless these are directed to God. Thus it is that the humble person feels saddened when he hears himself being praised, knowing that the praise and admiration that should be directed to God alone has been diverted to him.

Truly humble people do not compare themselves to anyone else, neither their superiors, nor their inferiors, nor their equals. They do not spurn anyone, nor do they presume that they see into the heart of any person, except for themselves alone. And they earnestly desire to be overlooked by others, and rejoice greatly when they do not receive any particular attention. The person who does not desire glory or praise from others does not fear gossip or slander.

But there are very many who make a show of putting themselves down and deprecating themselves, but inside they are full of falsehood.[4] As Saint Bernard observes, the truly humble person desires to be regarded as insignificant, but does *not* desire to be acclaimed and admired for being humble. The one who loves humility plants the roots of this humility in the depths of his heart. And this is done by recognizing honestly one's own fragility and weakness, by recognizing not only one's actual failings and sins but also all of one's *potential* failings and sins. Such a person sees that unless it was for the grace and protection of God, he could well have succumbed to innumerable temptations and sunk deeply into the most appalling depths of sin. For the potential to sin is within the fallen human nature of each and every one of us!

In this respect, each person will recognize his own fragility if he comes to know himself truly and honestly. If we each examine our hearts, do we not find a gaping abyss within them, a veritable whirlpool of vices and sinful desires? Thus it is written, "The source of your humility is within you."[5]

A good way of developing humility is frequently to undertake tasks and duties which are regarded as lowly or

---

[4]   See Ecclesiasticus 19:23.

[5]   Micah 6:14.

humble. For Sacred Scripture declares that a person will never arrive at humility if he flees from humble tasks.

No one is able to conquer temptations, either of the flesh or of the spirit, through his own efforts alone, but rather the grace of God is needed. Recognizing this reality always nourishes true humility. Similarly, we are not able to bring to completion any work that is good and pleasing to God unless we are helped by Jesus Christ.

It is an indication of humility if a person considers himself to be unworthy of any of the graces of God, and if he does not dare to aspire to any special spiritual gifts. Rather, the truly humble person is filled with awe and reverence when he discovers that God has poured out one of His graces upon him. The humble person would prefer to receive no graces of God at all than to receive a multitude of graces but fail to use them fruitfully. Sure signs of true humility are for an individual always to choose the lowest place, to associate with the least exalted persons, to prefer the humblest duties, and to dress in simple and unostentatious clothing.

Pride can be recognized by two kinds of signs. The first of these are its external manifestations, including a bold or flamboyant style of clothing, a grinning facial expression, and a swaggering gait.[6] Thus the good tree and the bad tree are distinguishable by their fruits. For all of our actions and

---

[6] See Ecclesiasticus 19:27.

external manners proceed from the thoughts and the inner dispositions of the heart, as Saint Augustine observes. A leering, bold, or lustful expression in the eyes expresses a proud and lustful disposition of the heart. And similarly, all external expressions come forth from and reflect a person's inner intentions.

Inner pride is revealed when a person places himself before others and expects to be placed before others, even though he may make an outward show of trying to please others, or may *seem* to wish to defer to others (especially those who are important or influential). Such behavior does not accord with the example given to us by Christ, our humble Master, who did not seek to please Himself but accepted the reproaches of others, which He did not deserve.[7] He did not come to lead but to submit, as He Himself declares: "The Son of Man came not to be served but to serve."[8]

Therefore, the teachers of others who do not follow the example of Christ but strive to win approval and adulation from human beings rather than from God waste the talents and virtues they have received. At last, such people shall be confounded because, as the psalmist testifies, "God shall surely spurn the proud."[9]

---

[7] See Romans 15:3.
[8] Matthew 20:28.
[9] See Psalms 52:6.

Prayer to God for Humility

O beloved Jesus, You are the eternal God, yet out of humility, You assumed the humble garb of our mortal flesh. And through this supreme act of humility, You became the supreme master and teacher of this noble virtue. Grant to me, O Lord, that I may obtain the hidden treasure of this holy doctrine, which You taught both by word and example. Pour forth into my heart, I pray, true and honest knowledge of myself, for this is the root and basis of all true humility.

Make me flee from all transitory honors, for honor and praise belong to You alone, not to me! May I cast myself at the feet of all my brothers and sisters and seek to be regarded as the least of all. For indeed, if it was not for Your grace and support, I should be the lowest and most vile sinner of all.

May my soul despise all vain pride. May I cast off all signs of this wicked vice, including the tendency to look down upon others and to compare myself with others in any way. May I become truly humble, and thus merit the consolation which You promise to the lowly of heart. Amen.

3

OBEDIENCE

True obedience to God exists when a person frequently and diligently tries to discern whatever is most pleasing to God in all circumstances and strives to fulfill with all his efforts whatever it is that God—who is wise and just and merciful—has ordained for him.

OBEDIENCE TO ONE'S SUPERIORS[10]

True obedience to the vicars of Christ (that is, bishops and religious superiors) exists when a person who is legitimately subject to such an authority obeys his directions faithfully and whole-heartedly, even when what he is asked to do runs contrary to his own inclinations. Such an obedient person will not show the slightest sign, either by his words

---

[10] In this section, Albert is primarily directing his counsels to professed religious, bound by a vow of obedience, and to clergy under obedience to a bishop. Nevertheless, many of the principles he articulates here can readily be applied to persons in different states of life (such as marriage).

or actions, that what he has been asked to do is contrary to his own inclination or preference.

But the genuineness of obedience cannot be fully tested or gauged, as long as it happens that the instructions given by the superior coincide with the preferences and desires of the subordinate. As Saint Augustine observes, "Your best servants, O Lord, are not those who hear You command them that which they already wish for, but rather those who wish for whatever it is that You command them."

The one who is truly obedient does not simply wait passively to receive orders before acting. Rather, once he knows the will and intention of his superior, he actively seeks out directions whereby he can put this will and intention into practice. This is in accordance with the example of our Lord Jesus Christ, to whom the will and good-pleasure of God the Father was itself His highest commandment.

The truly obedient do not choose their own actions for themselves, nor do they hasten to make their own judgments about matters, nor do they make a show of their own opinions before their superiors. Rather they accept legitimate directions openly, neither willing nor not willing anything for themselves. They are prepared to leave all decision-making to God and to their superiors in a spirit of openness and availability.

The truly obedient person does not even discriminate between what seems good and bad to him, in the same way that Abraham, when God commanded him to sacrifice his own son, did not judge the inherent goodness or badness of the action enjoined upon him. The truly obedient person is content to accept whatever is commanded of him as being for the best.

The exception to this is, of course, if something is manifestly and indubitably evil and contrary to divine law. In this case, it is prudent to consider the observation of Saint Gregory the Great, who declares obedience (if it is practiced as a genuine virtue) can never lead to evil.[11] However, at times it may sometimes lead to ceasing from one good work in order to do another good work.

Saint Gregory also observes, "Sometimes obedience will require of us things which are pleasing and in accordance with our personal desires, and sometimes it will ask of us things which are natural to our own preferences and desires. If one fulfills instructions in a way that is motivated by personal ambition or preference, then the virtue of obedience is rendered null. And if one does what is commanded when it is contrary to one's inclinations in a grudging or resentful way, then the virtue of obedience is diminished. Rather, for an act of obedience to be pure and perfect, it

---

[11] The implication of this is that if following the directions or commands of a superior ever led to an evil act or sin, it would not truly be the virtue of obedience at all, since it would be contrary to the more fundamental obedience to divine commandments.

should be done in a way that is unaffected by one's own preferences and desires. Obedience in doing difficult or unpleasant things becomes more glorious when one does it whole-heartedly, with one's will united to that of God. And obedience in pleasant or desirable things is more genuine when it is done without any thought for self-interest or one's own preferences but rather with a view only to the glory of God."

The supreme and perfect obedience of Jesus Christ should lead us to this true and pure obedience. For Christ not only obeyed God the Father in all things, declaring, "Let not my will, but Thine be done,"[12] but He even obeyed mortal beings with submission and meekness, and in one instance He even deferred to the request of a devil.[13]

Similarly, all created realities, both visible and invisible, are subject to God and should fittingly act in accordance with His will. Yet God has, in turn, made all created things to be subject to humanity. As examples of this, we may consider how the sun and the moon obeyed the words of Joshua,[14] and how the earth obeyed Moses when it swal-

---

[12] Luke 22:42.

[13] This seems to be referring to the incident in the exorcism of the Gerasene demoniac, in which evil spirits plead to be sent into some swine, to which Jesus agrees. (See Matthew 8, Mark 5, and Luke 8). Of course, though this request came from evil spirits, it did not actually involve any evil action.

[14] See Joshua 10:12–13.

lowed up Korah, Dathan, and Abiram.[15] The sea became submissive to the will of Peter while he walked upon it, and it was also obedient to the command of Moses when it engulfed and drowned Pharoah and his wicked host. In Egypt, serpents often obey the voice of the magicians and conjurers. And in the lives of the Desert Fathers, we read of wild beasts, such as lions and hyenas, following the orders of holy hermits. And demons submitted to the commands of the holy apostles, while birds obeyed the words of Saint Francis of Assisi.

Now, since other created things are thus subject to humanity, it follows that humanity should, in turn, be obedient to God. In this way, human beings, who possess natural dominion over all other created things, become obedient instruments and conduits of God's holy will for all of creation.

Saint Bernard of Clairvaux describes for us a good indication of genuine obedience in the following terms: the truly obedient make no delay in doing what is asked of them. They do not put things off until tomorrow, but act immediately. They prepare their whole being to do whatever is enjoined upon them—their eyes are ready to see, their ears are ready to listen, their tongue is ready to speak, their hands are ready to work, and their feet are ready to set out on a journey. Again, Bernard observes that the truly obedient person is ready to place his entire will at the disposal of

[15] See Numbers 16.

his legitimate superior. Thus he can authentically recite the words of the psalm, "My heart is ready, O Lord; my heart is ready!"[16] He can say with perfect sincerity, "Lord, I am ready to do whatever You ask! Just say the word, and I shall obey. I am ready to abandon all else to obey You, to serve my neighbors, to deny myself, and—if You should wish it—to rest in heavenly contemplation."

A sign of a lack of the virtue of obedience is when a person makes himself a judge and adjudicator over the directions his superior gives him, and constantly grumbles in his heart about what he imagines to be unfair or wrong. Such a person will look for excuses why he is unable to obey, or why he should not obey. After this, he will typically seek out subtle ways in which he can avoid doing what is asked of him, trying to find other supposedly more pressing responsibilities or obstacles.

This is certainly not what holy Abraham did when the Lord commanded him to sacrifice his most beloved, only-begotten son! Rather, he set out at once to ascend the mountain of the Lord, without hesitation or excuse, and to do the thing which was enjoined upon him, though it was so contrary to his inclinations. And it was through this humble, ready, and unquestioning obedience that he merited a great blessing from God, both for himself and for his innumerable descendants for all eternity.

---

[16] Psalms 107:2.

PRAYER TO GOD FOR OBEDIENCE

Lord Jesus Christ, You preserved perfect and immaculate obedience at all times, and laid down Your life itself in Your death upon the cross as an act of supreme obedience to the Father. O Lord, I implore You to grant me this same perfect obedience—that is to say, the grace whereby I may be ready to sacrifice my own will and preferences to Yours, and apply all my efforts and powers to the fulfillment of whatever it is which You will for me in all times and places.

Grant to me also, Lord, complete and simple obedience to all my legitimate superiors, obeying those whom You have established as Your ministers. Let me do this both in easy matters and in those which are demanding or arduous, both in things which are enjoyable and pleasant as well as in duties which are irksome and tedious. May I submit all my own personal preferences with simple and complete resignation.

O Lord, not only did You teach the virtue of obedience but You exhibited it perfectly in Your own actions. For You obeyed not only Your heavenly Father but even the injunctions and commands of lowly human beings, whose rightful King and Master You were. May I refrain from questioning and judging my superiors hastily. Save me from all wicked murmuring, resentment, and grumbling within my own heart. Rather, grant that I may obey whatever is legitimately asked of me with a free, happy, and holy will, and out of simple and earnest love for You, my Lord and Savior. Amen.

4

PATIENCE

True and perfect patience consists in the readiness to sustain difficulties, hardship, and injustices—not only when one deserves them, but even when they are completely underserved. Thus perfect patience was exemplified by blessed Job, who declared, "I have not sinned, and yet I see bitterness everywhere I look!"[17]

It is, of course, more difficult to tolerate hardships and injuries when one does *not* deserve them and is innocent of all fault. Nevertheless, having a clear conscience can sometimes impart a certain sweetness and serenity in enduring adversities and ill-treatment. And so Saint Peter exhorts us, "Let none of you suffer for being a murderer or a thief or an evildoer or an interferer in other persons' affairs."[18] But if anyone endures ill-treatment for being Christian, then he gives glory to God, in whose name he suffers. It is better to suffer for doing good then for doing evil. For

---

[17] Job 17:2.
[18] 1 Peter 4:15.

what merit is there in sustaining a beating if you deserve it for having done some wicked deed? But to suffer patiently for doing what is right is meritorious and pleasing in the sight of God.[19]

That form of patience is particularly praiseworthy which is ready to tolerate injuries quietly, not only from enemies, but even from those who are friends or are considered to be good people, and to tolerate suffering not only when one has done something wrong but even for doing good acts. The soul which bears adversities with patience in the midst of unjust circumstances is especially beloved by God and becomes like a lily among thorns.[20] Now, a lily, when it is pierced by thorns, loses none of its radiant whiteness, but it even emits its perfume more sweetly and more powerfully than before it was pierced. Thus it is with the soul which suffers unjust hardships. For it retains the brilliant hue of a pure conscience, but adds to it the sweet and holy fragrance of holy patience.

It is a sign of genuine patience not only to tolerate hardships and difficulties which come but even to desire them for the sake of the love of God. This is to follow the example of Jesus Christ, who (speaking through the words of the psalm) said, "My heart awaits for sorrow and misery."[21]

---

[19] See 1 Peter 2:20.
[20] Song of Songs 2:2.
[21] Psalms 68:21.

The truly patient soul will not murmur or grumble in the midst of adversities, following the example of Job, who refused to speak a word against God even when struck by dire misfortunes. Rather, he rejoices with a grateful mind, blessing equally the name of the Lord who "gives and who takes away."[22]

The genuinely patient person does not seek to excuse himself from injustice and calumnies but commits himself to God in all things, with confidence that God will vindicate his innocence in His own good time. Thus it was that when Jesus Christ was interrogated by Pilate, He offered no reply or excuse for Himself. The truly patient person does not complain about what he is called to endure, thereby seeking relief in expressing himself in complaints and expressions of suffering. Rather, he reveals his sufferings to God alone, until the faithful Lord Himself brings him spiritual consolation.

THREE CONSIDERATIONS TO CULTIVATE PATIENCE

There are three useful considerations that contribute powerfully to the cultivation of the virtue of patience. The first consideration is to recognize that because of our many sins and failings, we rightly deserve the most bitter

---

[22] See Job 1:21.

of punishments and that whatever sufferings we sustain during our mortal life serve to alleviate what is our due. The second consideration is to bear in mind how long-lasting and dire were the sufferings born by Christ, who was completely innocent, and that, in comparison, whatever we are called to endure is but light and passing. The third consideration is to recognize that God is perfectly just, and so whatever we suffer for the sake of His name, or whatever we suffer through no fault of our own, He shall certainly make generous recompense for. This recompense for suffering shall be the delights, happiness, and joys which await us in the next world. Thus it is that the apostle Paul confidently declares, "Whatever we suffer in the present life is light and momentary, compared to the sublimity of eternal glory prepared for us."[23]

A proof of true and humble patience is not to take revenge on those who cause our sufferings, even when the opportunity presents itself. This should go even so far as preventing others from acting on our behalf, following the example of David. For he prevented his soldiers from killing Shimei, who hurled stones and curses at him as he passed by, and called him a "man of blood."[24]

The truly patient person has no thought for revenge and retribution, but even prays for those who injure him. In

---

[23] 2 Corinthians 4:17.
[24] See 2 Samuel 16.

doing this, he emulates the example of Christ, who prayed for the forgiveness of those who crucified Him, and Saint Stephen, who prayed for mercy for those who stoned him. Such prayers are heard by God with great delight, and He never fails to answer them. Thus it was that the prayers made by David, Christ, and Stephen on behalf of their persecutors were all received and granted by God the Father.

A sign of a lack of the virtue of patience is when a person is quick to abandon whatever good works or acts of piety he could and should do as soon as he finds himself suffering any kind of hardship. To do this is to lose all reward from God, both for the good works themselves and for enduring adversity. And this attitude can very easily conceal itself in subtle ways. But it is in reality the most dangerous form of impatience there is. For by withdrawing itself from works of charity or acts of piety, the impatient soul seeks to avenge itself upon the innocent and merciful God.

PRAYER TO GOD FOR PATIENCE

Why, O Lord, am I so quick to complain whenever I suffer any injustice or insult, or feel that I have been judged unjustly? If I keep in mind how many times and how seriously I have offended You and sinned against You, then I shall realize that I truly deserve most of these things which I suffer in this mortal life, and even much more. Let me reflect frequently that it is Your great mercy, O Lord, which permits me to undergo the light and passing trials and adversities of this present life in order to avoid the immeasurably graver and longer-lasting pains of purgatory or hell!

Lord, bestow upon me strength and spirit so that I may bravely tolerate whatever afflictions I encounter; for without Your grace, my own fragile flesh is surely destined to fail. Help me to endure all false judgments, unfounded suspicions, groundless gossip, and unmerited injuries. May I quietly accept such sufferings without murmuring or interior complaint and resentment but rather find joy and peace in innocence and purity of conscience.

Keep me ever mindful of Your love and Your passion, and grant that I may be strengthened in my own patience by consideration of these. Make me even desire whatever cross You choose for me, knowing that to live and die while bearing my own cross is to live and die in union with You. Amen.

5

POVERTY OF SPIRIT

To embrace the spirit of evangelic poverty perfectly means to be ready to leave all things freely for the sake of God and to seek to possess nothing beyond the necessities of life. Indeed, the charism of poverty even extends to being willing to go without things which are necessary at certain times, for the love of God. Where there is not an actual lack of something which is wanted or needed, then the virtue of evangelic poverty cannot be fully active.

Thus it was that our Lord Jesus Christ sometimes lacked the necessities of life, such as when He and His disciples were without bread, while passing through a cornfield. [At that time, His disciples, to satisfy this lack of food, were compelled to pick the ears of corn to eat them.][25] At certain times, Christ also lacked clothing, such as when he was stripped of His garments before the cross (as Saint Bernard testifies). And He lacked even water to drink, as

---

[25] See Matthew 12 and Mark 2.

He hung upon the cross and cried out, "I thirst!"[26] And, while on the cross, He lacked also any place on which to rest His sacred head, in accordance with His own prophetic words.[27]

Alas, how often do we complain that we lack something when in reality we have more than we really need!

A person who is truly graced with the spirit of poverty desires no passing thing. Such a person will even decline to accept gifts offered to him, following the example of Elisha, who declined to accept what was offered to him by Naaman,[28] or Daniel, who refused the reward given to him by King Belshazzar.[29] The soul that cultivates evangelic poverty much prefers the glory of the kingdom of heaven than even the greatest earthly riches. And through poverty, he sees a means of imitating Christ more perfectly and more fully.

THREE CONSIDERATIONS
TO CULTIVATE POVERTY

According to Saint Bernard, there are three considerations which serve to lead us to value poverty. Nothing, he says,

---

[26] John 19:28.
[27] Matthew 8:20.
[28] See 2 Kings 5.
[29] See Daniel 5.

is more dear to God, nothing more beloved to the holy angels, and nothing is more fruitful for the human soul than to finish life in faithful obedience to poverty.

The same saint testifies that voluntary poverty pleases God. In heaven, there are infinite riches and glory, and endless length of life. But poverty cannot be found anywhere within that celestial realm. Thus it was necessary for Christ to descend to this earth as a human being in order to embrace the treasure of poverty which He so greatly loved and desired—for in this world, poverty may readily be had by anyone who chooses it. Now, the fact that Christ Himself sought out poverty in this manner should convince all of us that it is a thing to be greatly esteemed and sincerely valued.

Another consideration which should impel us to value voluntary poverty is that when Christ ascends to the glory of His throne of judgment at the end of the world, it will be persons of poor and humble background (namely, the apostles, who were fishermen) who will sit in judgment over a multitude of the rich and noble.

Oh, how meritorious it is in the sight of God to leave all things for Him, and to be willing to choose poverty for the sake of divine love! The person who does this places all his trust in God. And surely this same God in whom he trusts, and who is the omnipotent Lord of the universe, can minister to him the necessities of human life—which, if considered objectively, are nothing more than a little food once or twice a day. For God gives freely to all, even to His enemies, an abundance of what is necessary for life.

But these necessities of life are only very small things in the sight of God. His greatest gifts are the spiritual blessings and graces, which He can confer at any moment. And these He gives not to His enemies but reserves for those who love Him with all their heart.

An indication of a genuine spirit of evangelic poverty is to have no concern for transitory things but to commit oneself entirely to the care of God with confidence and simplicity. For God provides even to the birds of the air and the crawling things of earth all that they need.

It is illuminating to consider the case of crows born with white feathers. When they are chicks, such birds are rejected by the parents, who are, of course, black. Nevertheless, even when ejected from the nest, these white crow chicks can survive, fed by the bounty of God, on the nourishment contained in dew or on the flies and insects which they find. And once they grow a little older and become black, their parents again begin to feed them. All the while, the little birds never cease to cry out strongly, with full confidence in the bounty of heaven. [This is truly a wonderful example of the providence of God towards all His creatures!][30]

---

[30] This anecdote about white crow chicks reflects Albert's keen interest in natural science, and seems to be based on his own observations. In fact, white crow chicks (and even adult white crows) have been found to occur.

Evidence of a false or feigned spirit of poverty or avarice [in a professed religious] is to seek for that which exceeds necessity, and to accept eagerly any gifts which are offered. The person who accepts gifts from others often does so at the price of their own liberty, according to what the Philosopher[31] says, "To accepts gifts is to sell your freedom."[32] Indeed, Scripture similarly counsels us, "Do not accept presents too readily. For these can sometimes blind the eyes of the wise, and alter the decisions of the just."[33]

How can a person be said to have honestly embraced the charism of poverty if he does not wish to endure any shortages or occasional deprivations, and if he eagerly accepts all gifts that are offered to him and even subtly solicits them? How can a person be called a true lover of evangelical poverty if he gathers and stores up for himself anything more than the genuine necessities of life?

PRAYER TO GOD FOR POVERTY OF SPIRIT

Most kindly Savior, You are the God of ineffable majesty and infinite riches! Yet you became a poor human being for the sake of my salvation so that You could enrich me with the treasure of holy poverty.

---

[31] I.e., Aristotle.
[32] Because they may give rise to obligations on the person who accepts them.
[33] Deuteronomy 16:19.

O Lord, what is it that You sought in this world? What was it that You found here? What was it that You chose for Yourself? It was poverty! For You chose to be born in the poverty of the stable, and You chose to die in the poverty on the cross. And upon that cross, You did not possess even water to drink, and lacked even a place to rest Your head.

Teach me to follow Your example diligently so that I may strive to do as You did, O Lord, and to desire what You chose for Yourself. Let me embrace holy poverty joyfully and freely, and come to glory in the pain and deprivation of the cross.

My King, through Your grace, help me to bid farewell to all the empty glories and superfluities of this vain and deceptive world. When I find that I lack anything, let me rejoice in Your love, knowing that through holy poverty, I am able to emulate Your example more closely. May I never deceive myself, and come to mistake luxuries and excess for necessities. Let no solicitude for earthly things take possession of my heart, but rather may I be constantly mindful that in my true heavenly homeland, a superabundance of all good things awaits me.

May I seek spiritual gifts more than material ones, knowing that You confer Your spiritual graces only upon those who truly love You. Lord, impart to me a disdain for all passing things so that I may cling more firmly to the treasures which are eternal. Amen.

6

CHASTITY

Perfect chastity is not only to restrain the body from all acts of impurity but even to keep the soul pure from all lustful desires. An example of this is provided for us in the person of Sarah [in the book of Tobit], who says, "Lord, you know that I have never desired a man, and have kept my soul clean of all lustful impulses."[34] Indeed, chastity calls us to preserve ourselves not only from lustful impulses but even from the occasions which are likely to give rise to them. Hence it is that the same Sarah adds, "Never have I mixed with those who indulge in flippant playfulness, and never have I walked with those given to levity and foolishness."[35]

The person who has truly embraced the virtue of chastity is the one who chooses this state not for the sake of obtaining grace in the present life or even to gain eternal glory in the world-to-come but rather simply for the sake

---

[34] Tobit 3:16.
[35] Tobit 3:17.

of conformity to the beloved example of Jesus Christ. For He chose for Himself this same life of chaste celibacy.

The example of our Lord Jesus Christ, of His most Blessed Mother, and of the virgin saints ought to encourage us to love holy chastity. In the virgin saints, we witness holy souls who were ready to disdain the riches and glories of this present world, and even to lay down their very life in order to conserve their precious chastity for the Lord. Consider the noble lives and deaths of Saint Agnes, Saint Catherine [of Alexandria], and Saint Agatha! And there are innumerable other such saints who exemplify perfect chastity. Saint Jerome writes extensively of women who have given up their lives for the sake of preserving themselves from violation and dishonor, even amongst the ancient pagans.

Again, chastity produces the wonderful fruits of purity and liberty of soul. This also ought to encourage us to cultivate it diligently. And finally, Christ Himself promises particular glory to those who persevere in chastity. For He said, "To the one who conquers" (that is, to the one who overcomes the desires of the flesh) "I shall grant to sit with Me on My throne in heaven, just as I Myself have conquered and sit with My Father in His throne."[36] And Scripture assures us that, "purity makes one close to God."[37]

---

[36] Revelation 3:21.
[37] Wisdom 6:20.

PRACTICES TO CULTIVATE CHASTITY

There are several practices that promote and conserve chastity. These are moderate and sparing consumption of food, wearing of simple clothing, an avoidance of physical luxury, and (most of all) to flee from places and situations in which there is immodesty, or where lust is likely to be inflamed, either in oneself or in others. If Dinah, the daughter of Jacob, had observed this last counsel, she would never have been taken captive. For, through curiosity, this Dinah went forth to Shechem to see the women of that city, and so she became the victim of abduction and rape.[38]

Similarly, it is prudent to avoid all persons whose motives and intentions are suspect, and all places which are compromising. Women ought to view all men with a certain degree of caution. And similarly, men ought never to assume naively that the intentions of any woman are entirely pure. This is in accordance with the counsel of Saint Jerome, who says, "If you wish to preserve chastity, avoid the solitary company of women, even those who are of good conduct. Show them love through prayer and moral support, rather than through keeping company with them."[39]

---

[38] See Genesis 34.

[39] The advice and observations of this paragraph are not completely in line with contemporary thinking. Nevertheless, Albert's comments no doubt reflect his own observations of human behavior, and are not without a certain wisdom in particular cases.

The greatest guardian of chastity is to take one's delight in God alone. If you do this, all other possible objects of desire will seem less attractive. The one who has genuinely tasted the joys of the spirit no longer hungers after those of the flesh. The unfortunate converse possibility of this principle is noted by Saint Gregory, when he says, "The person who has been conquered by love of earthly things finds no delight in God."

For the human soul is never able to be without some desire or source of delight. We can either love those things which are lower or those which are higher. The more the heart aspires to the higher realities, the more detached it becomes from the lower things. And, conversely, the more it burns with desire for earthly things, the more tepid and feeble grow its aspirations for celestial delights. It cannot love both the things of earth and the things of heaven in an equal manner at the same time.

Proof of the perfection of the virtue of chastity is to withdraw the five senses from all physical pleasures. The person who has achieved perfect chastity will preserve his heart from all vain thoughts. He will not seek his happiness or satisfaction in the sensations of sight, nor taste, nor smell, nor touch; nor will he crave for the amusement of jokes and flippant conversations. For it is often out of such activities that the lusts of the flesh are spurred on.

A sign of a failure or deficiency in the virtue of charity is greedy over-indulgence in food and drink. Indeed, it was out of over-indulgence in drink that the nudity of Noah came to be exposed, to his shame.[40] And Lot, under the influence of intoxication, was induced to commit horrid acts of incest with his own daughters.[41] Thus it is that the apostle Paul counsels us, "Do not be overtaken by drunkenness, for from this lust arises."[42]

Similarly, a lustful or "roving" eye is a manifestation of a lustful heart, as Saint Augustine so wisely observes. In the same way, an impure heart shows itself in immodest and unclean words, an immodest mode of moving,[43] and a constant seeking after conversation with women. This is expressed in the book of Ecclesiasticus, in which it is written, "Many have perished on account of the beauty of women! And because of this beauty, the flame of lust has burned in the heart of many like a fierce fire."[44]

Injudicious and excessive interactions with persons of the opposite sex can easily imperil the virtue of chastity. This is especially so where people succumb to the dangerous habit of paying excessive attention to the appearance

---

[40] See Genesis 9:20–21.

[41] See Genesis 19.

[42] Ephesians 5:18.

[43] In Albert's time, it was believed that a person's moral character was manifested in their manner of standing and walking.

[44] Ecclesiasticus 9:9.

and physical form of members of the opposite sex. Thus it is that Ecclesiasticus warns us, "Do not stare at a young woman, lest her beauty become your downfall."[45]

All these counsels are of particular relevance to those who are bound by vows of chastity, and should be observed by such persons with particular care.

PRAYER TO GOD FOR CHASTITY

Lord, subdue in me all the wicked and disordered impulses of my senses. Cleanse my heart from self-will and from every impure thought. Grant to me a heart which is clean, pure, and enamored with Your own spirit of chastity, by means of which I shall be able to preserve my body and soul from all stain of corruption.

Grant that I may never fall from chastity, and help me to flee zealously even from the occasions of temptation. Bestow upon me the virtues of temperance and sobriety, a love of self-denial and penance, and mindfulness of my own fragility. With this fleshly fragility ever before my eyes, may I avoid all contacts and situations where my chastity of mind or body will be imperiled. For, truly, it takes but a single small spark to enkindle a raging fire! Above all, O Lord, let my heart be ever fixed upon You, for by experiencing the

---

[45] Ecclesiasticus 9:5.

sweetness of divine contemplation, all other allurements will lose their capacity to enthrall me.

Lord, lead me to appreciate Your immense beauty, generosity, and power, and to direct all my yearnings and desires towards that. O my King, Spouse of my soul, You have taught us to aspire to this noble virtue of chastity. Help me to imitate the glorious example of Your immaculate Mother and other virgin saints, who preferred to be parted from mortal life itself than to lose their purity.

But, Lord, I realize that without Your grace, I am utterly incapable of this. You ask of me chastity: firstly grant to me, I beseech You, the grace whereby I may be faithful to this intention—for without Your grace, I can do nothing at all! Amen.

7

ABSTINENCE

Abstinence shows itself to be true and perfect when a person is content with only what is necessary in both food and clothing, and shuns everything that is superfluous and serves merely for gratification. For such things, if pursued eagerly, take up much energy and effort and are attained only with considerable (and unnecessary) expense.

An example of the perfection of the virtue of abstinence can be seen in Saint John the Baptist. He lived off wild locusts and the leaves of a certain tree, the sap of which had the flavor and likeness of honey.[46] For drink, he took nothing other than water, and for clothing, he used the skin of a camel. This is in accordance with the words of the apostle [Paul], "Having food and clothing, let us be content

---

[46] This description of the "honey" which John the Baptist ate as being the sap of a certain kind of tree may well reflect Albert's own interest in natural science. It should be regarded more as an interesting speculation than a historical fact.

with these."[47] For the one who is a servant of God should not make use of clothing for the purposes of adornment or beauty, but simply for the sake of covering himself.

The true lover of abstinence does not refuse only those pleasures and delights that are prohibited to him, but he uses even those pleasures which are licit and necessary (such as food and sleep) purely for the sake of the love of God. If a person happens to delight more in drinking chilled water than in wine, it will be more pleasing to God for him to abstain from chilled water than from wine. If a person delights more in eating porridge than partridge,[48] it will be more pleasing to God for him to abstain from porridge than from partridges!

As Saint Augustine says, "If delicacies are consumed without particular desire, they do not offend." But even simple foods, if they are consumed with a desire for sensory gratification rather than an intention to nourish the body, may impair the virtue of abstinence. It is related that once when King David was desiring to drink water in an overly eager or gluttonous way, he poured it out rather than drinking it, as he felt his desire was greedy.[49] But Elijah, who had no desire to eat meat, was given it by God through the agency of a raven, and he did not hesitate to consume it.[50]

---

[47] 1 Timothy 6:8.

[48] The alliteration between porridge (*puls*) and partridge (*perdix*) is in the Latin text, which has a slightly humorous tone at this point.

[49] See 2 Samuel 23:15–17.

[50] See 1 Kings 17.

The virtue of abstinence involves not only restraining oneself from pleasures of the body but also from those of the heart and mind. Such things include all vanities, pointless and idle conversations, excessive joy in worldly success, and carnal friendships. This abstinence from the vain delights of the mind and heart is more praiseworthy in the sight of God than mere physical abstinence.

TWO CONSIDERATIONS TO CULTIVATE ABSTINENCE

There are two important considerations that promote the cultivation of the virtue of abstinence. The first of these is the realization that if we receive the gifts of God without sufficient gratitude, or if we use them in a way or for a purpose other than that for which they were intended, then we shall surely incur the wrath of God. The second consideration is that we shall be called to give an exact account of how we used all the resources and gifts with which God provides us. This means that we will have to justify and explain our use of them by showing that we employed them to serve some useful and proper purpose, or to fulfill some necessity, or for the common good. Now, the person who is abstemious makes use of few resources, and for this reason will have a much easier and simpler task to fulfill when he is called to give this account before God.

THREE BENEFITS OF ABSTINENCE

There are two wonderful benefits which emerge from the practice of abstinence. The first of these is that one becomes blessed with an insight into the divine mysteries; and the second is that one's prayers are heard more effectively and surely by God. Both of these benefits are demonstrated in the case of the prophet Daniel. When he was residing in the palace of the king of Babylon, he refused to accept the royal food offered to him but preferred to subsist on vegetables and water.[51] The first result of this was that he soon came to transcend all the magicians and sages in his interpretation of visions and dreams.[52] The second result was that his prayers were unfailingly answered by God. For example, in response to his prayers, King Nebuchadnezzar lost his senses and came to live in the manner of a beast for some seven years.[53] In another instance, he prayed that his people would be granted permission to return to Jerusalem, and indeed obtained this wish.[54]

Daniel was heard by God and his prayers were received favorably on account of the careful abstinence which he practiced. He himself testifies, "In those days, I, Daniel, mourned and wept for three weeks, and did not eat fine

[51] See Daniel 1.
[52] See Daniel 2.
[53] See Daniel 4.
[54] See Daniel 10.

bread, nor did any meat or wine enter my mouth, nor was I anointed with oil. And therefore the angel of God said to me, 'From the first day when you resolved in your heart to deny yourself in the presence of God, your words have been heard!'"[55]

There is also a third benefit resulting from abstinence—namely, that it is an effective means of procuring the mercy of God. This is illustrated in the case of the people of Nineveh. For after Jonah had warned them of their impending destruction, they undertook fasting and penance, and so were forgiven by God for their transgressions and their threatened doom was averted.[56]

We are able to marvel at the abstinence of many of the priests and saints of ancient times, but we cannot [and should not] imitate it. Of these, Saint Jerome writes that he always abstained from meat and wine. They did this on account of the tendency of such food and drink to arouse the passions and give rise to fleshly temptation.[57] They were even sparing in their consumption of basic necessities, such as bread, lest their spirits be burdened.

---

[55] Daniel 10:2–3, 12.

[56] See Jonah 3.

[57] In the ancient world, the consumption of red meat was often believed to increase the animal passions of the body. Eating red meat was also a less common practice in the ancient world than it is today (partially because of the cost of killing valuable working animals), and was therefore seen as a luxury item.

When they ate bread, they would often sprinkle it with crushed hyssop in order to increase its nutritional properties and make it more filling.[58] The only oil they consumed was that which came from [raw] olives—and they ate very few of these, of course, on account of the bitterness of their taste.[59] And need I say anything about the flesh of fowls? [Naturally, they were sparing even in their consumption of this.] They also avoided eggs and milk, considering these to be almost the same as meat. For eggs and milk may both be regarded as kinds of "liquid meat."[60]

A sign of true abstemiousness is when a person avoids all delicacies and fine foods when in good health, and even when he is in ill health. Thus when compelled by necessity

---

[58] Hyssop (of which lavender is a variety) was believed to have medicinal and nutritional value. Albert's comment is, literally, that it made the bread "heavier," but the English rendering given above conveys what seems to be his intended sense. The point he is making is perhaps that by adding hyssop to their bread, the ancient priests were able to retain health and strength, despite their abstemiousness in regard to the quantity of food eaten. Albert was keenly interested in the medicinal properties of herbs, and this comment reflects this.

[59] Olive oil was a standard part of the diet in the ancient Mediterranean world. However, raw olives (directly from the tree, without any treatment) are somewhat bitter to eat.

[60] Saint Albert the Great is not here advising a vegan diet but relating reports of the practices of some ancient monks and priests. Earlier, he has commented that while these examples are worthy of wonder and admiration, they cannot and should not be imitated (at least for most people).

to consume more delicate foods than usual, he does so for health reasons alone, and not for the sake of pleasure. Similarly, a person who cultivates frugality in consumption for the sake of the virtue of abstinence should give whatever becomes superfluous to himself to the needy. In this way, his abstinence will serve best to promote the salvation of his soul in a double sense—both by self-denial and almsgiving.

A sign of false or counterfeit abstinence is when a person makes a great show of denying himself luxuries which would not be readily available to him anyway. And there are those who publicly announce their acts of self-denial for the sake of gaining praise or commendation from others. And yet others deny themselves luxuries out of pure parsimoniousness or avarice, for the sake of saving themselves money. And there are those who follow a program of strict self-denial purely to attain physical health, beauty, and longevity, with no regard to its spiritual fruits whatsoever. While all of these examples are indeed forms of "self-denial," they cannot be equated with the virtue of abstention in its genuine, spiritual sense, since they are directed towards attaining passing and worldly goals rather than achieving future glory.

A PRAYER TO GOD FOR ABSTINENCE

Lord, teach me to shun all that is excessive and superfluous so that I may be content to have simply what is necessary, in food, drink, and clothing. May I learn to abstain not only from fleshly excess but also from all vain and empty gratifications and amusements of the heart and soul. Let not pleasure and self-indulgence be my rule of life but rather reason and necessity. I know that as long as I am filled with love of You alone, no other delight—whether lawful or unlawful—will ever be able to ensnare my heart and affections. But grant me prudence and moderation so that my cultivation of abstinence may not exceed the degree of stricture which is pleasing to You.

Mindful always that I shall have to render an account to You, O Lord, for how I have used all the good things which You have given me, may I make use of all things in accordance with reason, moderation, and necessity in perfect obedience to Your most holy law. Amen.

8

PRUDENCE

True and perfect prudence consists in constant mindfulness of the glories of the divine nature and an awareness of the wretchedness and limitations of our mortal condition. Saint Augustine eloquently expresses his own desire for this prudence when he implores the Lord, "O immortal and unchanging God, may I come to know You, and may I come to know myself!"

The person who possesses this true prudence seeks diligently to recognize those things which are most worthy of being aspired to and then works to attain them with all his heart. Similarly, he carefully considers what should be most carefully avoided and acts accordingly. The truly prudent person often reflects upon the future glory of heaven and the future torments of hell. Thus he recognizes how great a thing it will be to be united eternally with the highest and most perfect good, which is God Himself, and similarly, what a dreadful and horrendous thing it would be to be eternally separated from the goodness of God by mortal sin and eternal condemnation.

CULTIVATING PRUDENCE

The prudent person will carefully avoid everything that separates him from God, or makes him become distant from His supreme goodness. This includes venial sins, which distance the soul from God, or separate it from Him temporarily. He will also, of course, carefully avoid all mortal sin, which has the power to separate a soul from God eternally.

Similarly, he will diligently pursue everything which draws him closer to God—namely, good works and piety. And he will cultivate those things which, when fully and perfectly developed, bring the soul into complete union with Him—namely, the virtues and the gifts of the Holy Spirit.

The example of the philosophers of ancient Greece provides us with instructive lessons for the cultivation of true prudence, as Saint Jerome comments. For these ancient philosophers (though not enlightened by the Christian faith) nonetheless fled from human company and the distractions and temptations of cities and towns. For they believed that the abundance of luxuries and sensory diversions and attractions in such places could serve to weaken the soul and character, to undermine reflective thought and thus impair the development of true wisdom.

It is indeed an ill-advised course to be constantly surrounded by temptations and distractions, and to wish to gain experience or knowledge of things that would be better off avoided altogether.

The Pythagoreans made it their custom to live in deserted places. They carefully shielded their vision to avoid seeing those things which could distract them from the contemplation of philosophy.[61] If anyone imagines that he can indulge in an abundance of fine food and drink and be surrounded by luxuries and yet not be led into vices or assailed by temptations, then he is deceiving himself! Our minds naturally think about the things which we see, hear, smell, taste, and touch. And the desires and appetites of the heart become directed to those things from which we experience pleasure. If the ancient philosophers (who were pagans) recognized the importance of guarding the senses from distractions, how much more ought we (who are illuminated by the Christian faith) carefully shield ourselves from what is likely to tempt us into vice, or to generate within us unhelpful desires?

Another consideration which should lead us to the cultivation of prudence is the great number of people who have come to their downfall through foolishness. Hence we read in the prophet Isaiah, "My people have been taken captive,

---

[61] The Latin text here is: *"Quosdam legimus sibi effodisse oculos, ne per eorum visum a contemplatione Philosophiae avocarentur."* The sense has been slightly altered in the translation to make it more acceptable to modern sensibilities.

for they do not have wisdom!"[62] Similarly, in Baruch, "For these people do not have prudence, and so they shall perish as a result of their foolishness."[63]

The purpose of prudence is to order the thoughts of our hearts to ensure that they do not wander from God and what is rightly ordered towards God. This means that our attachments and affections should not become ensnared by created things, that our wills should not be diverted from what is pleasing to God, that our intentions do not become confused and polluted but are purified, and that our judgments and speculations are conducive to what is genuinely good.

Similarly, all of our words and actions should be correctly ordered and directed towards their proper purpose—that is to say, the promotion of justice and righteousness, and the common good. For, as Solomon testifies, "the wisdom of a person shines forth in his face"[64]—in other words, in his exterior actions. Hence it is that well-ordered actions and behavior are strong evidence of the possession of prudence. Saint Bernard counsels us, "Consider carefully your daily actions and conduct. Think about where you have succeeded or made progress, and where you have failed or struggled. What are your habits, and what are your thoughts and feelings? Are they similar to those of God, or unlike Him?"

---

[62] Isaiah 5:13.
[63] Baruch 3:28.
[64] Ecclesiastes 8:1.

O Reader, strive diligently to know yourself! For you will improve yourself more by knowing yourself well, than by knowing the course of the stars and the properties of herbs while remaining ignorant of your own soul.

A sign of false prudence is to labor to know the courses of the stars, the powers of herbs, the properties of gemstones, and so forth for the sake of worldly prestige or profit. Knowledge acquired with such a motivation does not edify, but rather puffs up.

Similarly, to be cunning in secular affairs and business is not a sign of genuine prudence. As the apostle Paul observes, "To be wise in the ways of this world is to be a fool before God."[65] And there are very many such people! Thus it was that the Lord Jesus lamented, "In this age, the children of this world are more astute than the children of light."[66] And there are many who are diligent in investigating vain and pointless matters and making new discoveries but remain completely blind as to the will of God. It is concerning such persons that the prophet Jeremiah wrote, "They are wise in doing evil, but ignorant about how to do good."[67] Such people, as the Apostle observes, proclaim and believe themselves to be wise, but in reality, alas, they are nothing but fools![68]

---

[65] 1 Corinthians 3:19.
[66] Luke 16:8.
[67] Jeremiah 4:22.
[68] See Romans 1:22.

A PRAYER TO GOD FOR PRUDENCE

May I know You, O Lord, and may I know myself! May I frequently meditate on those good and bad things which will remain with me after the end of this difficult but short mortal life; may I mindfully distinguish between the things of which You approve and love and those things which displease You. And may I flee whatever tends to separate my soul from You, but cling to whatever brings me into closer union with Your blessedness.

Even the pagan philosophers were able to cultivate and teach a disdain for the insubstantial pleasures and fugacious glories of this passing and inconstant world, since they recognized that such things could hold them back from contemplation of higher and more lasting realities. How foolish must I be if, enlightened by the truths of Christianity, I fail to be mindful of the smallness and insignificance of all created things in comparison to the infinite splendor and glory of You, their Creator!

O Lord, bestow proper order upon all my thoughts and feelings, and upon my will, intentions, judgments, words, and works. Direct all of these rightly—that is to say, towards Yourself. For You are the beginning, the center, and the end of all things, and in You, O Lord, rests the sum total of all my happiness. Amen.

9

FORTITUDE

Perfect fortitude is to be able to rule and govern well one's own soul. This means being able to restrain the soul from all pride, envy, wrath, lust, avarice, vainglory, self-satisfaction, and carnal desire so that the rational intelligence refuses ever to consent to or cooperate with such tendencies. Hence it is written, "The one who rules his own soul is better than the one who conquers cities!"[69]

It was this spiritual fortitude which Samson, who was otherwise so strong, did not possess. For though he killed a lion with his bare hands and slaughtered many people with the jawbone of an ass, in the end he was deprived of all his power through being overcome by the desire for a woman. Even holy David did not always possess this spiritual fortitude perfectly. For, even though he killed lions and bears and defeated the giant Goliath, he was not able to restrain his own eyes from temptation. Oh, how great

---

[69] Proverbs 16:32.

was his strength in undertaking fasting and works of penance! Yet despite this, he could not always keep himself from vices and temptations. In particular, he was not always able to restrain his tongue from speaking words of deceit and evil.[70]

The apostle James writes about the perils of unrestrained speech when he says, "All beasts, birds, serpents and other creatures are able to be tamed, but no person can govern the tongue! For the tongue is restless, and carries with it a lethal venom."[71] Nevertheless, unless one learns to control the tongue, there is no true piety possible. Accordingly, James elsewhere declares, "If anyone thinks himself to be religious, but cannot control what he says and deceives himself, then his religion is in vain!"[72]

The positive experience of spiritual delight is something which encourages true fortitude. This spiritual delight [which is sometimes experienced in prayer and contemplation] strengthens the mind to do good works, endure hardships, resist temptation, and conquer the vices. The strengthening effect of this spiritual delight is prefigured in the person of Jonathan, who, after tasting some honey, became energized

---

[70] This is perhaps a reference to where David attempts to manipulate Uriah in order to conceal his own act of adultery with Beersheba, Uriah's wife. Finally, David orders Uriah to fight in the most dangerous part of a battle in order to eliminate him. See 2 Samuel 11 and 12.

[71] James 3:7–8.

[72] James 1:26.

and invigorated in order to defeat his enemies.[73] And it is similarly prefigured in Moses, who, after experiencing the delights of conversation with God, was capable of maintaining a continuous fast for forty days.[74]

The purpose of the virtue of fortitude is to strengthen the mind in its knowledge of God, to impart vigor and constancy to one's love of God and neighbor, to give courage and endurance in the midst of adversities so that the will does not succumb to fear, and to confirm the heart in stability and humility so that it does not become foolishly or vainly elated in prosperity or success. It serves also to animate and encourage a person in doing good works, and to prevent him from becoming discouraged when things go badly.

A form of false or perverse fortitude is for a person to use his strength and courage for deeds contrary to the will of God. Saint Anselm observes that sinning is not true freedom, and generally does not arise from strength, ability or liberty, but rather from a deficiency in these things.

How perverse and deplorable it is, therefore, for people who actually have these good gifts—strength, ability, and liberty of soul—to use them to do what is contrary to the will of God! In fact, the misuse of this natural strength shall render them all the more culpable before the Lord.

---

[73] See 1 Samuel 14:24–45.
[74] See Exodus 34.

Thus it is that the prophet Isaiah writes, "Woe to you who are powerful in drinking wine, and strong in pursuing drunkenness!"[75]

It is this type of misdirected strength or perverse and false fortitude which animates those kings and princes who persecute the Church. And the Antichrist and his associates shall abound with a similar type of perverse strength!

A PRAYER TO GOD FOR FORTITUDE

O Lord, how weak and feeble is every mortal being who relies upon himself alone. But how strong are those who rely upon You! How strong is the soul that has once tasted the sweetness of Your spirit, both in performing good works and in enduring tribulation, in resisting the temptations of the flesh and withstanding the hard blows of adversity.

Lord, strengthen my soul with Your own fortitude so that it may be able to combat the sinful influences of the old Adam within me. Never let me consent to the insidious persuasions of temptation. Lord, bring my senses and my members (especially my tongue) under firm control, for without Your grace, I cannot succeed in taming them. And I know that if left ungoverned, they will surely flare up like a fire and become a font of a multitude of evils and ills.

---

[75] Isaiah 5:22.

Let neither adversity or prosperity sway me from what is right, Lord. Govern my inner heart, and let it not become fatigued in undertaking those things which are pleasing to You. Let me never shun difficulties and trials, for such things serve to nourish true and lasting fortitude and virtue—by means of which I shall be able to serve You ever more faithfully, my God. Amen.

10

JUSTICE

True and perfect justice consists in paying to God due praise for the splendor and glory of His divine nature. This includes giving to Him both fitting gratitude for all the good gifts which He bestows upon us, but also giving Him praise and glory for whatever sufferings we are called to undergo, according to the mysteries of His divine plan. It includes making due satisfaction for all our sins and shortcomings, either through what we do or what we fail to do, and also fervent and heart-felt sorrow for all the graces and gifts which we have neglected.

True justice in our relationship to God includes complete and unwavering fidelity to Him, including careful observance of all His commandments and all the obligations of our vows or religious commitments. It means undertaking all of one's duties with singular diligence, as if our whole salvation depended entirely upon each one of these duties, in a particular sense. Furthermore, to make our works pure expressions of our gratitude towards God, they should be done purely out of service to Him, and not to gain any human favor or approval. And all gifts from God should be received gratefully, and in such a way that they are used and enjoyed according to the ordering and purpose which God has assigned them.

TWO ASPECTS OF JUSTICE

Justice towards our neighbors has two aspects. The first aspect is never to do to one's neighbor what one would not want done to oneself. That includes never deliberately hurting or offending him by word, or action, or sign, or by plotting against him, never suspecting him of evil, never detracting from his reputation or disparaging him behind his back, and never trying to impede him from achieving any good thing. For there is no one who would justly wish such things to be done to himself, and therefore no one ought to do them to his neighbor.

The second aspect of justice to one's neighbor is to do for him what one would justly wish to be done for oneself. This includes treating him with due respect and courtesy and not thinking evil of him, rejoicing with him when he rejoices and sympathizing when he suffers, to assume his innocence, and to defend him from attacks when he is absent. For everyone would naturally and justly wish such things to be done for them, and therefore ought to do them for others.

Here, it must be emphasized that these two principles extend only to things which are in accordance with what is lawful and right. For example, a judge obviously would not wish to be sent to prison himself, but that does not mean that he ought not to sentence convicted criminals to prison—for that is required of him by law and his own official and legitimate duties.[76] Or a violent man may actually wish other people to challenge him to a fight, but that does not mean he should challenge others to fights—for, again, that would not be in accordance with what is right and lawful.

Justice towards the dead consists in observing and fulfilling any legitimate and reasonable intentions that they express in their will or last testament, and also offering prayers, fasting, and almsgiving for their souls. According to Saint Bernard, "The sufferings of those who are in purgatory are relieved or shortened by means of prayer, fasting, and almsgiving."

Justice towards the holy angels, and in particular towards one's guardian angel, includes following their counsels and guidance without hesitation and rendering them due praise and thanks for the many diligent services they bestow upon us.

---

[76] In the Latin text, it speaks of hanging a thief rather than sending him to prison. This reflects the practices and attitudes of Saint Albert's times but has been modified here to accord better with current thinking and sensibilities.

We ought to be encouraged in the cultivation of justice by the verse of the psalm of David: "The Lord is just, and He loves just ways."[77] Again, the just person is promised the rewards of joy and hope, according to the verse, "The just shall rejoice in the Lord, and shall find their hopes in Him."[78] The just person is also promised exultation and praise, as expressed in another psalm, "Exult in the Lord, O you just! For praise befits the righteous."[79] Finally, those who practice justice are promised eternal life itself, according to the verse, "The just shall live forever."[80] And, indeed, all the good things which are promised in Scripture are to be gained through the diligent cultivation of justice in every matter of life.

The function of the virtue of justice is to make all our thoughts and feelings rightly and properly ordered, and always in harmony with the will of God, so that our will conforms with the divine will, and our intentions are always directed towards the greater glory of God. Similarly, this virtue, when fully cultivated, causes all our words and actions to be directed towards an authentically just purpose, reflecting God's plan. Where this is the case, it is clear proof that the virtue of justice flourishes within a person's soul.

---

[77] Psalms 10:8.
[78] Psalms 63:11.
[79] Psalms 32:1.
[80] Wisdom 5:16.

But a sign of counterfeit or false justice is when a person usurps for himself things which properly belong to God alone, or usurps for himself things which belong properly to his neighbor. For example, the right to judge and to punish other human beings is the prerogative of God—for a private individual to do this is thus to usurp something which pertains to God [or the legitimate institutions of Church and state] alone.[81] And a neighbor's property and reputation belong to him and are his concern—to attempt to take them away from him is to usurp something properly belonging to someone else. As a warning and admonition against such false justice [which is the same as injustice], we read in the psalm, "O my God, direct my steps, so that injustice may never rule me!"[82]

A PRAYER TO GOD FOR JUSTICE

Lord Jesus Christ, You are perfectly just, and You Yourself are our justice. Grant to me Your grace so that I may render to You the sacrifice of praise which is Your just due. And truly, it is right and just that You should be offered my expression of praise and gratitude, on account of both all the

---

[81] From Saint Albert's earlier comment on the duties of judges, he clearly regards the official judicial and penal process as being a legitimate part of God's plan.
[82] Psalms 118:133.

benefits that You have graciously and generously bestowed upon me and all the bitter sufferings that You bore for the sake of my salvation.

May I weep contritely for the many sins and offenses that I have committed against You, and also for my negligence and indolence in the proper use of the gifts You have granted me. May I remain faithful always to my own vows and commitments and to all Your commandments, O Lord.

Let me never do unto my neighbor what I would not want done to myself, for this is the foundation of all justice. Make me treat with justice also the faithful departed, offering prayers and penance for the remission of their sins and their admission into eternal rest. And, finally, make my soul obedient and attentive to the counsels and admonitions of my guardian angel. For it is indeed just and proper that I should exhibit humble reverence and obedience to this marvelous spiritual protector and guide, who is so diligently solicitous for my welfare and salvation. Amen.

11

TEMPERANCE

True and perfect temperance is the just and ordered governance of both the interior movements of the heart and of exterior actions.

The person who possesses true temperance not only restrains his mind from all evil and useless cogitations and desires, but even carefully moderates his good and useful thoughts to keep proper measure in them. For, indeed, sometimes excessive occupation with things which are in themselves good and valuable can lead to a distraction from proper duties. An example of this would be a person attending divine worship who finds himself preoccupied with thinking of his other duties (even though those other duties may be good and useful in themselves). As Saint Bernard says, "The one whose mind is occupied with other things during the liturgy, and so not paying attention to what it should be focused on, will not receive the Holy Spirit. For God wills us to make our thoughts and intentions accord with whatever He has ordained as proper at any given time."

Similarly, the person who has acquired the virtue of temperance perfectly will be able to govern not only his thoughts but also his feelings and affections. Thus he will neither hope for nor fear anything beyond the extent that it is proper for him to hope or fear, and he will neither rejoice nor mourn over anything beyond what is fitting. Similarly, feelings such as love, hate, and shame, will all be kept in their proper and appropriate measure.

Temperance includes being able to govern the mind so that it does not allow itself to become occupied with some intellectual matter for longer or with greater intensity than it ought. The will should also be regulated so that one wishes for things only to the extent that it is proper and fitting to wish for them, and in a way that accords with the purpose which God intends for them.

The truly temperate person will be able to control his tongue and be able to speak or to keep silent as the occasion may require. Control of speech goes beyond merely what one says but also extends to the choice of people with whom one converses, and the times and places when one speaks. All speech should be carefully considered and directed either to some necessity or some useful purpose.[83]

---

[83] Clearly, the display of sociability, courtesy, and friendliness would be considered as "useful purposes."

The temperate person will likewise have good control over even the movements of his body so that, as the Apostle says, "All things may be done decently and in order."[84]

We should be encouraged to cultivate the virtue of temperance by the example of Divine Providence itself, which ordains all things in an orderly way and has organized the things of the created world according to determined measure, number, and weight. Following this example, we should also govern our own actions, habits, and lives with due measure, number, and weight. There are three elements that reflect the Holy Trinity itself—with *measure* pertaining to the omnipotent virtue of the Father, *number* pertaining to the eternal wisdom of the Son, and *weight* arising from the inspiration of the Holy Spirit.[85]

Similarly, the example and teachings of the apostle, Saint Paul, exhort us to temperance. For he said, "Strive to offend neither the Jews nor the Gentiles nor the Church of God; just as I myself endeavor to please all, not seeking what is useful for myself, but what will promote the salvation of

---

[84] 1 Corinthians 14:40. As noted previously, in Albert's time, posture, style of walking, and facial expressions were all considered to be signs of a person's moral character.

[85] This Trinitarian attribution of measure, number, and weight is not explained here, and how Albert arrived at it is not entirely clear. Aquinas quotes Wisdom 11:21 using these three to denote God's Goodness (*ST* I, q. 5, a. 5).

many."[86] Saint Paul truly exemplified the virtue of temperance, striving to offend no one, but rather to render himself acceptable and respected by all. He did this not for his own personal advantage but for the purpose of spreading the Gospel more effectively and more credibly.

True temperance shows itself in moderation in food, clothing, and sleep. The temperate person treats all of these in such a manner that they adequately fulfill all that nature requires. But he does not allow himself to exceed the necessities of nature to any great extent, lest he drift into superfluity and luxury. For the things of nature are given to us to be used to fulfill the needs of nature, and not for the purposes of self-gratification. Such self-gratification always proves vain, for it never leads to genuine happiness or satisfaction, and is very often the occasion for sin.

The truly temperate person endeavors to preserve measure in all things. The only exception to this is the love and praise of God. For the Lord is infinite in His glory and perfection, and therefore the love and praise that is due to Him is correspondingly infinite. For this reason, it is fitting to love God without measure or restraint. But, apart from God, all other things should be loved only in their due measure.

A sign of intemperance is when a person is unable or unwilling to conform himself to prevailing customs and

---

[86] 1 Corinthians 10:32–33.

expectations. Such a person is unable to restrain his own desires and preferences, and thereby becomes incompatible with all others. Thus Saint Augustine wrote, "You, O Lord, have declared that every soul which lacks self-control soon becomes a burden to itself, and so it is." And, as much as intemperate people are burdensome to themselves, they are even more so to others! An example of this is in the character of Ishmael, of whom it is written, "He was a fierce and wild man. His hand was against all others, and the hands of all others were against him!"[87]

A PRAYER TO GOD FOR TEMPERANCE

My God and Creator, You have made all things in proper and admirable number, weight, and measure. Grant that I may do all things with attention and circumspection so that I may likewise act in accordance with the correct ordering of things, observing their proper number, weight, and measure.

Govern my heart, O Lord, lest it drift into useless and disordered thoughts. Do not permit me to become excessively preoccupied with anything at all, even matters and concerns that are useful and good in themselves. Temper the affections of my soul so that I may neither love nor hate anything in a way that exceeds due proportion. Let me

---

[87] Genesis 16:12.

neither rejoice nor be saddened beyond the measure that is fitting and rational.

Assist me to restrain my tongue so that I may judiciously either keep silence or speak in proper measure. Let me not indulge or delight in food, clothing, sleep, or any other material comforts excessively, but be content with what is necessary and shun all superfluity.

Lord, graciously bestow upon me the virtues of temperance and moderation. Let me preserve measure in all things—with the single exception of my love, praise, and gratitude to You, O God; for in this alone is no measure or restraint needed! Amen.

12

COMPASSION

True compassion in relation to God is to feel constant and sincere compunction in one's heart for all the injuries that are done to Him, and are still being done to Him and His Church, and also to those who love Him. For God feels such closeness, care, and sympathy for those who are beloved by Him and who love Him, as much as a person feels for the pupil of his own eye. And all the elements of the universe (even those which are inanimate and non-sentient) shared in the appalling sufferings of Christ upon the cross, [thereby exemplifying the compassion due to God, their Creator].

True compassion towards one's neighbor is to feel sympathy in one's very bones for all his sufferings, both physical and spiritual. This is exemplified by the apostle Saint Paul, who said, "Who is there who suffered, with whom I also did not suffer?"[88] The *Glossa Ordinaria*[89] comments on this

---

[88] 2 Corinthians 11:29.
[89] The *Glossa Ordinaria* was a standard commentary on Scripture in general use amongst theologians and scholars at the time of Albert.

verse, saying that when Paul says this, he means, "Who was there who did not feel weakness in their faith, or in any other virtue, for whom I did not feel compassion? That is, I felt their pain and struggle as if it were my own. And who was there who was offended or scandalized, for whom I did not burn with the fire of compassion?"

Our duty of compassion extends also to our brothers and sisters who are in purgatory. We should share in their sufferings in our own hearts, especially for the fact that they do not yet enjoy the vision of God in all its fullness and glory. It is fitting that we constantly intercede with God for these suffering souls, that He may deign to give them relief from the severity and bitterness of their afflictions and may shorten the time of their purgation.

The overflowing compassion of Christ should encourage each of us to cultivate this virtue. As Saint Augustine observes, Christ hastened always to relieve sinners from the torments of their conscience, and felt the sufferings of others with more intensity than He felt His own. And it was not merely a *feeling* of sympathy with the pain of others—rather, He literally took our sufferings and sorrows upon Himself, for, as the prophet Isaiah eloquently testifies, "ours were the sorrows He bore; ours, the sufferings He carried."[90]

The realization that we are all members of the same body should also encourage us to feel compassion towards others.

---

[90] Isaiah 53:4.

The apostle Saint Paul offers us this analogy: "Just as when one member of the body suffers, so do the other members suffer with it."[91]

Compassion achieves a double purpose: it confirms the virtue of charity and it advances our sharing in the kingdom of God. Regarding this first purpose, in the book of Ecclesiasticus we are urged, "Do not withhold your compassion from those who weep, and walk with those who mourn. Do not disdain to visit the sick. Through these actions, you shall be confirmed in love."[92] Regarding the second purpose (that is, of becoming sharers in the Kingdom of God), the Apostle writes, "If we sustain [others in compassion,] then we shall surely reign with Him."[93]

But despite this, the virtue of compassion is rare. Thus it is that we hear the voice of Christ lamenting, through the words of the psalm: "I suffered and endured, but there was none who shared my sorrow. I sought for one to console me, and found no one!"[94]

---

[91] 1 Corinthians 12:26.
[92] Ecclesiasticus 7:38–39.
[93] 2 Timothy 2:12.
[94] Psalms 68:21.

SIGNS OF TRUE AND FALSE COMPASSION

A sign of true compassion is not only to share the sufferings of one's friends but even to sympathize with one's enemies. Thus it was that Joseph wept for each of his brothers in their need and affliction, although they had previously sold him into slavery.[95] And King David wept with great sorrow over the death of Saul, who had often tried to kill him while he lived. Indeed, David even composed songs of mourning for the Israelites over the death of Saul. David showed similar compassion for his son Absalom, even though he had tried to usurp his kingdom from him. For when Absalom died, David mourned with genuine sorrow, "O Absalom, my son Absalom! How I wish I could have died in your place! O Absalom, my son Absalom!"[96] And Job also testifies about the depth of his compassion, saying, "I wept even over the one who was afflicted, and my soul was moved with pity for the poor."[97]

A sign of false or counterfeit compassion is when a person offers words of sympathy and makes a show of sorrow in his face and yet feels secret gladness in his heart over the affliction of his neighbor. Another sign of a lack of

---

[95] See Genesis 42:24.
[96] 2 Samuel 18:33.
[97] Job 30:25.

compassion is when a person is able to easily alleviate the suffering of others but does nothing to do so.

A PRAYER TO GOD FOR COMPASSION

O Lord, Your compassion is vaster and more profound than anything that we could possibly imagine or hope for. Through this divine compassion, You took our sufferings and sinfulness upon Yourself in Your agony and death upon the cross.

Through that same compassion, I beseech You, O Lord, transfix my own heart with sorrow and penitence for all the innumerable sins and offenses I have committed against You and against all Your servants in this world. Let me be moved to sincere compassion for all the sufferings of body and soul that afflict my neighbors; may I share in their pains as if they were my own, for we are all limbs of one and the same body. May I constantly be mindful of the fact that all human beings are brothers and sisters, for we are each the offspring of the same celestial Father.

Let my compassion extend to the souls in purgatory, especially those whom I have known and loved during this life. May I endeavor to relieve their pains by means of my own prayers and works of penance so that they may quickly come to behold the wonders of Your glory, who live and reign forever and ever. Amen.

13

PEACEFULNESS

True peace with God consists in placing all of one's abilities, and all of one's actions and thoughts, and all the powers of the five senses entirely at the disposal of God's will. This entails governing one's thoughts, feelings, desires, and intentions, as well as all exterior actions, in such a way that they are ruled by reason, and this reason, in turn, must accord with the will of God. All actions, thoughts, and impulses which do not accord with reason inevitably result in a disturbance to both exterior and interior peace.

True peace with one's neighbor means sincerely trying to avoid doing anything that will disturb their peace. Indeed, whoever deliberately disturbs the peace of another always loses his own peace as well. For the one whose peace is disturbed will try to vindicate himself, or, if he is not able to do this, he will bear hidden ill-will in his heart. And the person who is responsible for disturbing the peace of another will find that the reproaches of his conscience steadily gnaw away at his own peace of mind.

The person who is a sincere seeker after peace will focus his intentions and judgments upon the condition of his own soul rather than those of others. He will be ready to put aside his own opinions in favor of those of others, and will put aside all preoccupation with worldly and exterior matters in favor of the internal contemplation of the glory of God. For in God alone is true peace to be found! Saint Augustine famously testified to this, when he wrote, "You made us for yourself, O Lord, and our hearts are restless until they rest in you."

The virtue of peacefulness possesses a twofold usefulness, which should greatly encourage us in its pursuit and cultivation. First, the cultivation of peace produces a delightful state of calmness and serenity of mind. And this delight, which can be experienced in this life, is a foretaste of the eternal sweetness and delight of the kingdom of heaven. Second, God is able to prepare for Himself a dwelling-place only in the soul which has made itself peaceful and calm. For the Lord declares, in the words of the psalm, "In peace shall I take my rest."[98] Similarly, in another place, we read, "In peace shall He make His dwelling-place."[99] The apostle Paul encourages us to cultivate peace, saying, "Have peace, and the God of peace shall be with you!"[100]

---

[98] Psalms 4:9.
[99] Psalms 75:3.
[100] 2 Corinthians 13:11.

SIGNS OF GENUINE AND FALSE PEACE

A sign of the virtue of genuine peacefulness is for a person to avoid all places and interactions that are likely to lead to disturbance or unrest.[101] Another sign of peacefulness is for a person to hold himself firmly to the commandments of God in every time and place. For, as the psalmist states, "There is great peace for those who love Your Law, O Lord."[102] The subjection of the impulses of the flesh to the spirit in all things is also a sign of, and a factor contributing to, genuine peace.

An indication of a deficiency in the virtue of peacefulness is not to be able to detach oneself from the sources of disturbance and agitation. Such persons cannot renounce their self-will, nor their aspirations to distinguish themselves from their peers, nor their desires for pleasure.

There is a kind of "false peace" which some people experience at times. This false peace does not come forth as a result of their own virtue but rather as the result of the actions of others and the external circumstances they find themselves in. For example, there are many people who seem to be peaceful, but this is only for as long as they encounter nothing contrary to their wishes. And as soon as

---

[101] Albert is not here advocating fleeing from all possible situations of conflict, but rather prudently avoiding what seem to be likely occasions for profitless disturbance.

[102] Psalms 118:165.

anything happens which does *not* accord with their wishes or does not please them, their apparent peacefulness immediately vanishes. In such cases, they never really possessed the virtue of peace at all, but, rather, they benefited from that virtue in others. For this reason, their apparent peacefulness can easily be overturned by external changes.

But the person who possesses the virtue of true peace will not be disturbed in the least by what others may do or say. He will neither be elated by praise nor dejected by criticism. On the contrary, his inner peace will remain secure no matter what happens—since such peace depends not on the actions of others or external circumstances but only on his own inner virtue, through the grace of God.

A PRAYER TO GOD FOR PEACEFULNESS

O Lord, You are the true Solomon or "King of Peace," and You Yourself are our peace. You are the still center of heaven and earth. You are the highest and perfect good, in which alone can our minds find complete and lasting serenity.

Lord, gather together all the conflicting and battling parts of my soul, which have been dissipated and divided by the multitude of trials and temptations of this passing and ever-fluctuating world. Grant that they may be unified and reconciled in love of You alone, and thus bestow upon me that peace which only You can give.

Bring my will into harmony with Your will so that I may desire nothing but what You desire. And let my body be brought into obedient and peaceful submission to my soul.

May I emulate the bee which works diligently and assiduously within its own hive but is not concerned for anything external. May I thus cultivate virtue in my heart and not concern myself with judging others. And teach me to avoid all occasions that are likely to bring nothing but profitless perturbation.

Let my peace be founded on nothing but You, O Lord. In this way, I will cease to depend upon what other people do or say for my own peace but rather will find secure peace in my own faith and will become a source of peace to my brothers and sisters. Amen.

14

MERCY

The virtue of mercy comprises three elements in its practice: giving, forgiving, and accepting forgiveness.

The truly merciful person will give to those in need, as long as he possesses anything himself. In giving, mercy has not reached its perfection until you have given all that you can afford to give. The blessed Job possessed this mercy in giving in exemplary fashion. For he said, "My door never remained closed to the pilgrim or wayfarer, and I never caused the widow to depart with a downcast eye. Never did I enjoy my food alone, while an orphan went hungry. For mercy has always been with me, from the day when I first came forth from my mother's womb."[103]

But merely *giving* from one's possessions, without *forgiving* offenses that one has sustained, is not enough to count as true mercy, as Saint Gregory the Great argues. The genuinely merciful person forgives injuries and

---

[103] Job 31:32, 16–18.

offenses he suffers willingly, before his forgiveness is even requested. He never seeks revenge, either through himself or through the agency of another. Thus it is often the case that a merciful person is more ready to forgive than a guilty person is to apologize. The truly merciful person will feel greater sorrow for the sin that has been committed than for any injustice that he himself endures. Thus it was that David, when Shimei cursed him and hurled stones at him, did not take revenge upon him, and even prohibited his soldiers from taking revenge on his behalf.[104] And thus it was that Joseph showed mercy to his brethren, who had sold him into slavery, by weeping sincerely over each one.[105]

But even willingly forgiving those who have done wrong is not the perfection of mercy. For the perfection of mercy extends to praying to God that He may forgive those who are guilty of the offense which one has suffered. Thus it was that Moses prayed to God for mercy for those who had attempted to stone him to death, saying, "Lord, forgive them for this sin; or, if You will not forgive them, delete me also from the Book of the Living, which You have written."[106] And Saint Stephen, the protomartyr, also prayed to God for mercy for those who were stoning him, and Christ Himself prayed

---

[104] See 2 Samuel 16.
[105] See Genesis 45:15.
[106] Exodus 32:31–32.

for those who had crucified Him. Both implored, "Father, forgive them, for they know not what they do!"[107] Their mercy thus went so far as to attempt to excuse those who cruelly killed them, before the divine justice of God the Father.

The consideration that God Himself is supremely merciful ought to encourage each of us to the diligent cultivation of mercy. Moreover, God's merciful nature causes Him to love especially those who show mercy to others, as Christ's words demonstrate: "Go forth and learn mercy, for it is mercy which I desire, not sacrifice."[108]

Another motivation towards cultivating mercy is that God, whose nature is merciful, will judge without mercy those who have not shown mercy themselves. We read this in the epistle of the apostle Saint James, who writes, "There will be judgment without mercy for those who have not been merciful to others."[109] But God will display the fullness of His own mercy to those who have been merciful themselves. As the book of Proverbs testifies, "He who has mercy upon the poor makes a loan to God."[110] In other words, whatever one has given to others—either in generosity or forgiveness—shall be repaid by God with abundant interest.

---

[107] Luke 23:34; see Acts 7:60.
[108] Matthew 9:13.
[109] James 2:13.
[110] Proverbs 19:17.

SIGNS OF TRUE AND FALSE MERCY

A sign of true mercy is when a person gives all he can to those in need, sparing only enough to provide for the necessities of life, and works industriously not to enrich himself but to be able to support the poor more generously.

Evidence of a lack of mercy is when a person has the means, resources, and opportunities of helping those who are in need but chooses to ignore them, or, like the hypocrite described in the letter of Saint James, says to them, "Go in peace, keep yourself warm and eat well!" but then does nothing to supply them with what they need.[111] Accordingly, Saint John Chrysostom exhorts us, "Do not be stingy with what you possess. For everything that you seem to possess is really only entrusted to you on loan by God—why, then, should you cling to it as if it were really your own?"

Again, other signs of false mercy include when someone apparently forgives those who have wronged him but only because he has no means of taking revenge, or when he forgives them but not out of genuine mercy but only because of fear of the judgment of God, or when he forgives others in words only but still carries a grudge against them in his heart.

---

[111] James 2:16.

A Prayer to God for Mercy

O Lord, why is it that we human beings are often so tenacious and avaricious in clinging to the things of this world, which are only ever passing and incomplete? Those who appreciate Your own merciful generosity in giving to us everything which we possess will not hesitate to convey this merciful generosity to others, through their own free giving of what You have given them. For in doing this, they will surely obtain Your mercy all the more abundantly.

Pour forth, O Lord, Your mercy into my heart so that I may be ever ready to assist the poor and the needy. And when I do not possess the resources to assist others in need, at least give me generosity of heart to give them my prayers, love, and goodwill.

In Your mercy, teach me not only to give but also to forgive. With my eyes fixed upon Your infinite love and the sufferings You endured for the salvation of the human race, help me to emulate Your own unbounded mercy.

Whenever I suffer an injustice, let me be more grieved at the sin and fault that has harmed another person's soul rather than at any loss or offense which I myself have sustained. And may I not pray for retribution for myself but rather that Your mercy may flow forth freely for the reconciliation of all the world. Amen.

15

CONCORD

True concord with God means to unite one's will to His, both when things are going well and equally so when they are going badly, and to strive to conform one's actions completely to the example of Jesus Christ. Hence Saint John Chrysostom wrote, "Nothing is more fitting and worthy than that human beings should strive to imitate their Creator, and, according to their own abilities, try to carry out the divine will of the One who made them. The Lord Himself desired this union when, towards the end of His earthly life, He prayed, 'Just as You, Father, are in Me, and I am in You, so may all of these be made one in Us!'"[112]

True concord towards neighbors emerges from sensing within them those things of God, and seeing within them the image of God. Just as in the early Church, it was said that "all were of one heart and one soul,"[113] for all were united in their faith and love for God.

---

[112] John 17:21.
[113] Acts 4:32.

Another sign of concord is to conform oneself with one's neighbor, in all those things that are not contrary to God nor one's particular vows or vocation. This includes a general conformity with prevailing customs in matters of food, clothing, sleep, conduct, and work.[114] It is in accordance with this principle that the apostle Saint Paul wrote, "We are made weak with the weak, that we may gain the weak for the Kingdom of God. Indeed, we make ourselves all things to all people, so that many of them may be saved."[115]

We should be encouraged to the love of concord by the fact that it is praiseworthy and pleasing in the sight of God. The words of Solomon testify to this, where he observes, "There are three things which are pleasing to God and approved by mortals: concord amongst brothers and sisters, love of neighbor, and a husband and wife who get along well."[116] The example of the holy angels, who are always in the most perfect peace and harmony, should also motivate us to cultivate concord with diligence. For by emulating their harmoniousness, we emulate also something of their heavenly beatitude.

---

[114] Albert is not here advocating unthinking or blind conformity, of course, but only a general observance of customs in matters which are not contrary to Christian morals or principles. A refusal to follow local customs, a tendency often referred to as "singularity," was seen as disruptive, especially for those in communal religious life.

[115] 1 Corinthians 9:22.

[116] Ecclesiasticus 25:1–2.

The fervent desire of Christ Himself to achieve reconciliation, both between God and the human race, and also among human beings, ought also to inspire us to seek to promote concord. For example, when the apostles contended among themselves about which of them should be regarded as the greatest, and when the other apostles became indignant at James and John for seeking places at His right hand and left hand, the words of Christ served to reestablish concord and harmony among them.

SIGNS OF TRUE AND DEFICIENT CONCORD

A sign of a genuine concord and harmony with God is to have a conscience that is untroubled with any sin. Examples of this can be found in Saint Paul, where he says, "My conscience does not accuse me of anything,"[117] and also in the holy Job, who says, "My heart has never reproached me for any crime throughout my entire life."[118] Such was his fervent desire to make progress in all the virtues that he never ceased to strive to do good works, according to the will of God!

A sign of true concord with one's neighbor is never to raise any complaints against them, nor ever to participate in any grumbling or gossip about them. The genuine lover

---

[117] 1 Corinthians 4:4.
[118] Job 27:6.

of harmony will never speak a word of disparagement or detraction against anyone. The parents of Saint John the Baptist, Elizabeth and Zechariah, were wonderful examples of concord both with God and with their neighbors. For they are described as "following all the commandments and ordinances of the Lord," and also as being "without complaint."[119] Another noteworthy case of a person exhibiting concord both with God and neighbor is Judith, of whom it is written, "She was highly regarded and admired by all, for she sincerely feared the Lord, and there was no one who spoke any word of ill against her."[120]

But a sign of negligence of the virtue of concord is when a person does not examine his own conscience carefully or honestly. When this happens, such people often imagine that they are at perfect peace with God and their neighbor, when, in reality, this is not the case at all.

Another sign of a lack of concord with God is when a person finds the divine commandments displeasing, or even dares to disagree with the official teachings of the Church. It is about such persons that it is written, "The one who is displeased by God is displeasing to God!"[121]

---

[119] Luke 1:6. The expression "*sine querela*" (literally "without complaint") in Luke 1:6 is normally translated as "blamelessly" in English versions of this text, but Albert clearly has its literal meaning in mind here.

[120] Judith 8:8.

[121] Albert does not give a source for this quotation. It may have been a proverb or popular saying at the time.

A sign of a failure of the virtue of concord in an individual is when he finds good actions and upright moral character displeasing and annoying; even though he may sometimes praise them verbally.

Yet another indication of a lack of the virtue of concord is for a person always to believe his own judgment is superior to those of others, and also when a person deliberately cultivates opinions and views that are out of harmony with his peers.

A PRAYER TO GOD FOR CONCORD

Grant me, O Lord, the grace of concord and conformity with Your will. Help me to desire always whatever it is which You desire, both in times of prosperity and times of adversity. May I strive to imitate the model of Your own divine and heavenly conduct, to the extent that I (a wretched mortal creature) am able, by sedulously conforming myself to the example of Your beloved Son, Our Lord Jesus Christ.

Make me also cultivate concord and harmony with my fellow human beings, endeavoring never to give just cause of complaint, or to give rise to needless dissention amongst them. Rather, [following the example of Saint Paul,] may I try to be "all things to all people," insofar as I am reasonably able, in order to win their souls over for Your kingdom.

Assist me to see clearly and honestly into the hidden corners of my own heart, lest self-love and presumptuous over-confidence ever deceive me into thinking that my works or life are pleasing to You, when, in fact, they may well be highly displeasing.

Let my concern always be to amend my faults and to perfect my virtues, and to submit myself willingly and joyfully to Your mandates. For in this submission, I know that I will come to enjoy the blessed fruits of holy concord, both with Your holy will, O God, and with my brothers and sisters. Amen.

16

CONSTANCY

Perfect constancy exists when a person is not able to be deterred or distracted from his faith, devotion to God, and commitment to sound morality and upright conduct by anything that happens to him, no matter how good or bad.

Thus it was with Job, who declared, "Until the day I die, I shall never depart from my innocence, nor shall I abandon the righteousness to which I have committed myself."[122] Neither the temptation of good things nor the hardships of tribulations and calamities were able to induce Job to waver from his fidelity to the divine commandments. It was similar with the seven brothers in the book of Maccabees, who were tortured by having their tongues cut out and the skins on their heads removed, and then being immersed in boiling oil. Yet, despite all these horrendous tortures, they refused to be swayed from their commitment to God.[123]

---

[122] Job 27:5–6.
[123] See 2 Maccabees 7.

And Eleazar, the faithful elder, preferred to be flogged to death rather than to consent to eat unclean food.[124]

The person with true constancy in his faith will never cease from praising the glory of God, as is expressed in the psalm, "I shall bless the Lord at all times, His praise ever on my lips."[125] Nor will the constant person ever give up on his desire to make progress in the spiritual life, just as Pope Leo [the Great] once said, "There is no person who is so perfect and holy, that he cannot become more perfect and holy." And similarly, it is said that whoever no longer aspires to improve himself is in danger of going backwards.

The example of the constancy of the courageous and faithful martyrs should encourage each of us to strive towards this virtue. In particular, the virgin martyrs are wonderful examples, for they attained to eternal glory through their unwavering constancy, despite being of the more fragile sex.[126]

We should also be moved to firm constancy by the stubbornness and pertinacity of heretics, who, for the sake of adhering to their pernicious errors, suffer pangs of remorse and punishment in this life, and will undergo much greater torments in the next. [If such heretics are able to show such

---

[124] See 2 Maccabees 6:18–31.
[125] Psalms 33:2.
[126] This reflects attitudes towards gender differences which were generally accepted at the time of Saint Albert.

strong endurance all for the sake of vain errors, how much more ought we be able to remain unwavering in the face of adversity for the sake of the true faith?][127]

SIGNS OF TRUE AND DEFICIENT CONSTANCY

A sign of true constancy is when a person does not cease from doing what he knows is pleasing to God, even in the face of physical sufferings or loss of possessions. Thus it was that Tobit continued with his practice of burying the dead, even though the evil king Sennacherib confiscated all his wealth for doing so, and then commanded that he should be killed.[128] Thus it was also with the apostles, who did not cease from preaching the Gospel, even in the face of persecutions of all kinds. Accordingly, Peter and John asked their enemies, "You yourselves judge if we should or should not obey God! Do you really believe it is more just in the sight of God to obey you rather than to obey God?"[129] Similarly, Peter and the other apostles declared to those who opposed them, "It behooves us more to obey God than human beings."[130]

---

[127] This last sentence is an editorial addition. It seems necessary to complete the point which Albert is making here.
[128] Tobit 1:20–22.
[129] Acts 4:19.
[130] Acts 5:29.

A sign of a deficiency in the virtue of constancy is when a person withdraws from what he knows to be right for the sake of human favor or worldly profit. An example of this is Balaam, who wished to curse the people of Israel for the sake of gaining the favor of King Balak.[131] Another case is the rich young man, who departed sorrowfully from his determination to follow the Lord Jesus because he feared the loss of his material possessions.[132]

But a fine example of constancy is Saint Paul, who could not be swayed from his faith and vocation by any danger, perils, or threats whatsoever. Thus it was that he announced, "I am ready not only to be bound but even to die in Jerusalem for the sake of the name of the Lord Jesus!"[133]

A Prayer to God for Constancy

What will it benefit me, O Lord, to have begun my life with holy intentions if, as soon as some tribulation arises, I fall away from my good works? How easily I am tempted by worldly delights, and deterred by fear, and deceived by false hopes and vain ambitions! Why do the examples of so many courageous martyrs fail to move me to emulate their

---

[131] See Numbers 22–24. In the biblical text, it is not clear that Balaam actually wished to curse the people of Israel, but this is clearly Albert's interpretation.
[132] See Mark 10 and Matthew 19.
[133] Acts 21:13.

noble constancy? When I see how firmly many sinners and heretics cling to their vices and errors, how is it that I am so weak in clinging to what I know to be the truth?

Grant me constancy, Lord, and bestow upon me the firmness to adhere to what is right and just, even to the point of death. For without Your grace, I am weak and vacillating, but by virtue of the strength only You impart, I can withstand any temptation or trial. Amen.

17

GENEROSITY

Generosity reaches its perfection when a person is willing to give all that he can afford to give to assist those who are in need, and does so with joy and contentment. Indeed, such perfect generosity not only includes material possessions but also extends to the giving of spiritual benefits. These spiritual benefits include a willingness to listen to others, to proclaim the Gospel, to explain the teachings of the Church in a sound and knowledgeable manner, and to provide wise counsel.

This form of generosity should not be confined only to those who request such things but also to those who do not request them and even (on occasion) to those who do not care to receive them.[134] This is reflected in the exhortation of the apostle, Saint Paul, who said, "Preach the Gospel, both in season and out of season!"[135] Indeed, he

---

[134] Clearly, the offering of spiritual advice and teaching to those who have not asked for it or who are not willing to receive it must be governed by prudence, courtesy, and humility.

[135] 2 Timothy 4:2.

poured our tears and prayers for those who scorned the message of salvation. Likewise, the truly generous person will give of himself without reserve, in the form of private prayers, supplications, and tears, in order to promote the salvation of others.

We should be encouraged in the cultivation of a generous spirit by the example of God Himself. For He continually bestows the good things of creation and all the spiritual gifts necessary for salvation upon all the human race, good and bad alike. What is more, He gives to us even the very flesh and blood of His most beloved Son, our Lord Jesus Christ. Such is the immense and unfathomable generosity of God that it is not sufficient to Him to give all the good things of creation, but He bestows even His very self upon us!

The person who is willing to give to all alike according to their need, even to his enemies and rivals, demonstrates himself to possess in full the virtue of generosity. Indeed, the truly generous person will take special care to ensure that he does not exclude those who have offended him from his willingness to give.

When a person is fully infused with the virtue of generosity, he will barely be able to restrain himself from giving whenever he perceives a need or appropriate opportunity. This extends especially to the giving of spiritual benefits, such as by offering wise counsel and teaching the Christian truth. And he will do this even when he senses that by offering such spiritual gifts, he may make himself unpopular or become the target of persecution.

We should also be encouraged in our cultivation of generosity by realizing that whatever we give is not really ours at all. Rather, it all ultimately belongs to God, and we are merely acting as his stewards. In this, the popular saying applies: "The one who gives away a leather shoelace is not giving away a piece of their *own* skin."[136] Thus Saint John Chrysostom explains, "To ask you to give what is really your own would be to ask something difficult. But all that you have is God's, and has been loaned to you for a short time. Why, then, do you cling to it so tenaciously?"

SIGNS OF TRUE AND COUNTERFEIT GENEROSITY

A sign of true generosity is joyful giving without any hope of reward or recognition, and without any consideration of whether or not the recipient is deserving. Thus it was that Jesus Christ gave Himself and His all to us, and to all humanity. And in Christ we find the most perfect example of generosity. For His generosity extended even to giving

---

[136] In Latin, this proverb is "*Latae corrigiae scindantur ex pellibus alienis*" ("The shoelaces which are given away are cut from the skin of another"). This may be a translation of a vernacular saying in circulation at the time.

His very life for us, as Saint John recalls: "In this, we see the love of God, that He laid down His life for us; and so we also ought to be ready to give up our lives for our neighbors."[137]

Bishops are bound by this precept to an even greater degree than others. The apostle Saint Paul was a fine example of this, for he said, "I give all that I have to you without reserve, and I give my very self as well for the salvation of your souls."[138] Similarly, in another place he writes: "Each day I die for your glory, my brethren"[139]—meaning that, each day he is in peril of death for the sake of promoting the faith.

The truly generous person offers all that he has and all that he can do for the Lord without any hope of a reward. He does this not for any personal benefit, but purely for the sake of adding to the eternal praise of God, the exultation of the saints and angels, the conversion of sinners, the strengthening and encouragement of those who are righteous, and the remission and alleviation of the sufferings of those who are in purgatory.

A sign of counterfeit generosity is when a person gives only in order to win the praise and approval of others, or to avoid being perceived as stingy and selfish, or to silence

---

[137] 1 John 3:16.
[138] 2 Corinthians 12:15.
[139] 1 Corinthians 15:31.

those who are asking them to give. Such giving does not reflect the virtue of real generosity, and gains no eternal reward whatsoever.

Similarly, giving in order to gain favor from someone else, or to place another under an obligation towards oneself, is not real generosity. Even giving which is done purely in the hope of securing the reward of future glory or out of fear of being condemned by the Divine Judge, who commanded us to give, does not truly amount to the virtue of genuine generosity, since it contains an element of self-interest—although it does remain a meritorious act.

A Prayer to God for Generosity

O Lord, You are infinitely and unimaginably generous, for You confer to all Your creatures not only existence itself and all that is necessary for their survival but also give the gift of Your very own Self. Grant me the grace to imitate Your wonderful and selfless generosity to the extent that I am able.

You exhibit generosity in a particular way to human beings, Lord, for You gave Your own flesh and blood to them as food in the most holy Sacrament of the altar. And You generously opened the font of heavenly mercy to all persons—even to Your enemies and persecutors.

If You, Lord, are so generous, why should I not also strive to give freely? For everything which I *seem* to possess is not truly my own at all, but Yours. O God, I consecrate all that I have and my very being to Your love! May I recognize that in giving to my brothers and sisters in need, I am really giving to You, and I am giving to You only what is already rightfully Yours. Through doing this, may I come at last to that wonderful salvation and glory which You so generously purchased for me at the price of Your own precious blood. Amen.

18

TRUTHFULNESS

Genuine truthfulness is when the mind, the tongue, and the actions of a person concord perfectly. In such a case, the movements of the heart will be honestly reflected in the utterances of the mouth, and the person's actions will similarly match perfectly whatever words he has spoken. The perfectly truthful person, of which Saint Paul was an example, can honestly say "Just as I believe, so I speak and so I act."

The truthful person will carefully fulfill whatever he has promised or vowed, either in the sight of God or before his fellow human beings, and his actions shall always live up to his words.

The only permissible exception to this is when a wiser counsel deters a person from an original ill-conceived or poor intention, as Saint Isidore of Seville advises: "If you have made an evil or ill-conceived promise, you should take it back, or if you have sworn some wicked vow, you should revoke it."

We should be led to a love of truthfulness by the consideration that Christ Himself is (according to His own words) the Truth.[140] Furthermore, truth is always loveable in itself—hence, all persons naturally value and desire the truth. Even if the truth may be uncomfortable or difficult to endure at times, this is not because of an aversion to truthfulness itself, but because the realities which such truthfulness reveals are uncomfortable and difficult to endure.

The truth, in itself, is chaste, humble, and loveable, just as the Truth, in the person of Christ, commended chastity, humility, and charity to us. Pride is the natural enemy of truthfulness, whereas humility is its natural companion.

Furthermore, we should be drawn to aspire to truthfulness because of the fact that truth conquers all things. Because truth, in its highest sense, is immutable and indestructible; as our Lord Jesus declared, "It is easier for heaven and earth to vanish than for one stroke of the Law [which is the truth] to pass away."[141] And similarly, in the Gospel of Matthew, we find it written: "Amen, I say to you! Until heaven and earth have perished, not one dot, not one iota of the Law shall pass away, until all has been fulfilled."[142]

---

[140] John 14:6.

[141] Luke 16:17.

[142] Matthew 5:18. In these cases, the "Law" referred to is understood as indicating truth in a higher or spiritual sense rather than the regulations of the Torah.

SIGNS OF GENUINE AND DEFICIENT TRUTHFULNESS

Evidence of the virtue of truthfulness is when a person does not deviate from the truth, even for the sake of gaining someone else's favor, or his own personal convenience, or to prevent loss of possessions, or even injury to his own body. Neither will he seek to dissimulate or cover anything up. A genuinely truthful person will be careful not to utter a single word that conveys falsehood; nor will he retract anything which he has previously said, or withdraw from anything to which he has previously committed himself in his words, unless compelled by some unavoidable and ineluctable necessity. A striking example of this last characteristic of perseverance in the truth is demonstrated in the person of Balaam, who said, "Even if the king Balac were to offer me his palace, filled with gold and silver, I would not be able to change the words of my Lord! And I would not add to, nor take away from, anything I have already said."[143] Similar examples of adherence to the truth in the face of adversity are to be found in Jeremiah, Micah, Daniel, and the other prophets. These holy men could not be overcome by any opposition or threats whatsoever, and refused to deviate from the truth in either their words or their actions.

---

[143] Numbers 22:18.

A sign of a deficiency in the virtue of truthfulness is when a person expresses one thing with his mouth but has something quite different in his heart. Such a person will often change his words very easily, and for a slight or trivial cause. This is because the one who transgresses the truth moves into the realm of falsehood. And falsehood, by its very nature, is insubstantial and unstable, and therefore subject to causeless change and ceaseless fluctuation.

Similarly, the person who does *not* speak the truth openly when it behooves him to do so, or who does not defend the truth when he ought to do so, becomes, effectively, a traitor to the truth.[144] A priest, for example, has received the truth from God, and therefore he is duty-bound to defend the truth in the face of attacks and oppositions. Likewise, even laypersons, insofar as they have received and understood the truth through the instruction of the Church, are duty-bound to defend it in the face of opposition and misrepresentation.

---

[144] It is important to note Albert's qualification of the duty of speaking the truth *when it behooves a person to do so.* Clearly, a person is not bound to express the truth openly in all circumstances (such as by giving a negative opinion on another person's work or character when there is no useful reason for doing so, or by disclosing private, confidential, or irrelevant information).

A Prayer to God for Truthfulness

Lord Jesus Christ, You proclaimed Yourself to be the Truth, and You truly are the Truth itself. For the truth is immutable, unchangeable, and invincible, and thus mirrors the splendor and simplicity of God.

Help me to attain to perfect truthfulness so that my thoughts, words, and actions operate in perfect concordance and harmony. Let not fear, or the desire for benefits for myself, or any other consideration make me be led astray in falsehood. Let me seek to deceive no one, lest I end up deceiving myself.

Grant to me also discretion and prudence to discern when it behooves me to speak and when it behooves me to keep silence—for the perfection of the virtue of truthfulness consists in speaking the truth in the right manner and the right time. And let my heart be so conformed with the truth of Your Gospel that my every word, action, and thought may proclaim it authentically and boldly. Amen.

19

GENTLENESS

True gentleness is in its essence the same as *benignity*, or kindness. It abounds when a person does not permit his mind to become inflamed by injuries or injustices which he has suffered. The truly gentle person does not let any bitterness of heart he may feel manifest itself in his judgment or external actions. Rather, he is like the one described in the psalm, who "has ears but does not hear, and in whose mouth no reproof is to be found."[145] These words, of course, pertain particularly to Christ Himself, who (according to Isaiah) "did not open His mouth. As a sheep He was led to the slaughter; and like a lamb in the presence of its shearer, He remained silent, not opening His mouth."[146]

Thus we read in the *Glossa Ordinaria*[147] upon Matthew, "A person may be described as 'meek,' when he is not

---

[145] Psalms 37:15.
[146] Isaiah 53:7.
[147] The *Glossa Ordinaria* was the standard commentary on the Scripture during the scholastic period.

affected by bitterness of heart or hardness of mind, but accepts all things in the simplicity of faith." The meek person displays neither rage nor wrath nor rancor, but sustains all things with equanimity.

The Lord offered Himself as a teacher and exemplar of this noble virtue, and He would not have done this unless He knew that this is the most wonderful and consummate virtue, embodying all the others. Thus Christ said, "Learn from me, for I am meek and humble of heart."[148] The gentle person does not show any irritation or anger. He does not injure anyone, nor does he plot about how he can hurt others. The meek person is the one who is not swayed by violent passions and malicious thoughts, but has achieved victory over all disturbing emotions and aggressive impulses.

We should be inspired with a love of the virtue of gentleness by the words of Christ. For He promised, "Blessed are the meek, for they shall inherit the earth."[149] Concerning these words, Saint Augustine wrote, "I believe that the 'earth' of which Christ spoke here is the same as that which is referred to in the psalm, 'You are my hope, Lord, in the land of the living.'"[150] Similarly, Scripture testifies in another place: "The gentle shall possess the earth, and will delight

---

[148] Matthew 11:29.

[149] Matthew 5:4.

[150] Psalm 141:6. The word translated here as "land" (*terra*) is the same as the word translated as "earth" in Matthew 5:4.

in an abundance of peace."[151] Accordingly, "the gentle will hear and rejoice!"[152]

SIGNS OF AUTHENTIC AND COUNTERFEIT GENTLENESS

A sign of authentic gentleness is when a person, in the face of some hardship or adversity, does not murmur or offer any bitter words, either in his spoken words or even in his thoughts. And if he *does* feel any hurt or pain in his heart [which is unavoidable from time to time], he does not let it show in his facial expression, or words, or actions. Rather, he strives to keep his soul tranquil and quiet in order that it may be a fitting dwelling place for God at all times.

But a sign of counterfeit gentleness is when a person offers kindly and meek words, and displays a placid expression but, within the secret chamber of his heart, he knowingly and deliberately cultivates animosity and bitter thoughts.[153]

---

[151] Psalms 36:11.

[152] Psalms 33:3.

[153] There is a subtle but very important distinction between this and the previously described case. For, in the first case (of the truly gentle person), although the person feels hurt and pain in his heart, he does not *cultivate* any bitter thoughts (even though some bitter thoughts may arise without his consent). In the second case (of counterfeit gentleness), a person does not display anger in his words or actions but still actively and willingly cultivates bitter thoughts in his heart.

A Prayer to God for Gentleness

Lord Jesus, You called us to learn from You, "who are gentle and lowly of heart." And You taught this not only by precept but also by example. For You did not retaliate against those who insulted and persecuted You, but remained like a gentle lamb before its shearers. May I imitate Your example and fulfill Your teachings, casting off the bitterness of irritation, aggression, and belligerence, and clothe myself instead in the white robes of gentle meekness.

You have promised the meek that they shall inherit the earth. With my eyes fixed firmly upon You, most gentle Jesus, may I come to be numbered amongst the truly gentle who shall receive this glorious inheritance of rejoicing eternally in the land of the living, with You, who live and reign forever and ever. Amen.

20

FAITH

True faith is firmly to believe in the Father, the Son, and the Holy Spirit, and to believe that these are the one and only God, and to believe that in these three persons is a single, undivided Deity, equal in glory, and coeternal in majesty. Each person of the Trinity is truly Lord and God: uncreated, infinite, eternal, perfectly good, wise, and omnipotent. But there are not three Gods and three Lords, as if there were three beings who were uncreated, infinite, eternal, perfectly good, wise, and omnipotent. Rather, there is one God and Lord only, who is uncreated, infinite, eternal, perfectly good, wise, and omnipotent.

Amongst the three persons of the Trinity, there is none who is before or after any other, for they are coeternal. Neither is there anyone who is greater or less than the others, for they are equal in all things and coequal in perfection. Nevertheless, they differ in those characteristics which constitute their unconfused personhood. For the Father is unbegotten, and has no origin. The Son is begotten of the Father, as light from light, and true God from true God. The Holy Spirit is not created, nor is He begotten, but proceeds equally from both the unbegotten Father and the only-begotten Son.

Authentic faith commands us to believe that our Lord Jesus Christ is both truly God and authentically human. He is eternally begotten of the Father, according to His Divinity, and born of His holy Virgin Mother in time, according to His humanity. In His Divinity, He is coequal with the Father, but He assumed human flesh through the most pure blood of the Blessed Virgin Mary. According to His Divinity, He is immortal and impervious to suffering; yet according to His humanity, He was able to suffer and to undergo death. Genuine faith accepts all of these mystical paradoxes without any hint of hesitation, nor any shadow of doubt.

We should be encouraged in the cultivation of the virtue of faith by the venerable example of Abraham, Isaac, Jacob, Moses, and the other ancient patriarchs. Further encouragement is offered to us in the example of those who were gentiles and pagans by birth and upbringing, yet nevertheless committed themselves fully to belief in the Divine mysteries—such as Job of the land of Uz, or Rahab the prostitute, and many others. By faith, such persons become acceptable to God. But without this faith, it is absolutely impossible for anyone to be pleasing to the Lord.[154]

---

[154] See Hebrews 11:6.

Faith possesses a twofold usefulness. Firstly, if a person is filled with faith, all that he asks for he shall receive. Our Lord Jesus Christ Himself is a witness to this, for He declares, "All things are possible to those who believe."[155] And again, we read, "All that you ask for you shall receive, as long as you believe!"[156] And similarly, Christ declares, "If anyone says to this mountain, 'Cast yourself into the sea!' it will be done, as long as he does not doubt in his heart, but only believes."[157]

SIGNS OF GENUINE AND COUNTERFEIT FAITH

A sign of genuine faith is the regular undertaking of good works. For just as a body is dead without the spirit, so "faith without good works is similarly dead."[158]

But a sign of counterfeit or illusory faith is when a person does not really believe the Scriptures with all his heart. Often, a person with weak faith will believe that things happen through mere fate or chance, or through the course of nature, rather than through the providence of God.

Another sign of weak faith is when a person does things in private which he would not dare to do in public. For this

[155] Mark 9:22.
[156] Mark 11:24.
[157] Mark 11:23.
[158] James 2:26.

is a sure indication that he does not really believe that there is a God who is watching all his actions, whether they are done in private or public.

A Prayer to God for Faith

Lord God, You are mysterious and ineffable in Your nature and transcend all human comprehension. Therefore You may be known and loved, not by rational understanding, but by faith alone.

It is such faith which bestows power and efficacy to prayer, for You, O Lord, have assured us that any supplication or petition uttered with perfect faith will always be heard and answered. Fill my heart with the virtue and grace of faith, dispelling from me all presumptuous doubt, and helping me to believe even when I cannot understand. And let my faith be made living and true by the solid testimony of good works. Amen.

21

HOPE

True and perfect hope is the certain expectation of future beatitude. This certain expectation springs from the grace of God and is confirmed by preceding merits and good works. Both of these are necessary for true hope to exist. For the grace of God, which is freely given, cannot be preserved without the merit of actions. But, without this grace of God, no one may achieve salvation by their own merits and good works alone.

The person with true hope will frequently and diligently apply himself to good works. But he will not place his confidence in his own merits and efforts, but rather solely in the superabundant grace of God. For no person may know or presume with certainty that his own works are sufficient to please the Lord, since Scripture tells us that all human justice and goodness is but "filthy rags" compared to the perfect and ineffable goodness of God.[159]

---

[159] Isaiah 64:6.

Those who are infused with the virtue of hope strive always to offer a "just sacrifice" to God, in accordance with the verse of the psalm: "Offer a just sacrifice, and place your hopes in the Lord."[160] What is this "just sacrifice," one may ask? It is nothing other than our Lord Jesus Christ Himself, the only-begotten Son of God. For He is the One who offered Himself upon the altar of the cross, as the "just sacrifice" for the sins of the world.

Indeed, such is the unfathomable magnitude and infinite value of this sacrifice that it surpasses the value of the whole universe. As Saint Augustine has said, a single drop of Christ's precious blood would suffice to redeem the entire human race. And yet this blood (of which but one drop would suffice for our redemption) flowed forth in abundant torrents in order that the ineffable depths of Divine love might be fully revealed to us!

In this sacrifice is all of humanity's hope, both for mercy and for final beatitude. This is reflected in what Saint Bernard once said: "I have sinned with a very great sin. My conscience is troubled, but I do not despair; for I call to mind the power of the wounds of my Savior!" For Christ endured these wounds purely for the redemption of our souls from sin, and to secure for us eternal happiness. What is there which is so dreadful, so wicked, so lethal, that it cannot be overcome by the wounds of Jesus, and His most holy death upon the cross?

---

[160] Psalms 4:6.

When such a potent, efficacious, and beautiful remedy comes to my mind, I am not terrified by anything—neither the dread shadow of death nor the malignity of my own sins. Truly, Cain erred most greatly when he said, "My iniquity is greater than that I may deserve pardon."[161]

A little later, [Saint Bernard writes,] "What I find to be absent from my own self, I will find within the heart of Jesus, for from that heart flows forth a superabundance of mercy. Nor is this divine heart closed—for it has been wounded deeply, and through those wounds the streams of salvation gush forth. They pierced His hands and His feet with nails, and opened His side with a lance. And thus it is that I am able to draw forth honey from the stone and oil from the rock; so that, in accordance with the prophetic words, I am able to 'taste and see the goodness of the Lord.'"[162]

[Saint Bernard again writes,] "The nail which penetrates His flesh becomes for me a key,[163] unlocking all the treasures of the Divine will. The nail cries out, the wound cries out, 'Behold, the Divinity of Christ, reconciling all the world to Himself!' Thus the hidden mysteries in the heart of God are revealed through the wounds upon the sacred body of the Son; thus His ineffable mercy is made manifest

---

[161] Genesis 4:13. The sense of this is given according to the Vulgate text.

[162] Psalms 33:9.

[163] There is a play on words in the Latin text, with the word for "key" (*clavis*) resembling the word for "nail" (*clavus*).

to us, like the glorious and golden light of the dawn sun, arising from the eastern horizon!"

This most noble and perfect love of our Lord Jesus Christ should encourage us all in the cultivation of the virtue of hope. And this great and all-conquering love can in no way be doubted when we consider the bitterness of the pains which He willingly underwent for the sake of our salvation.

And, as further tokens of that same love and so that we should never lose this salvation won for us at so immense a price, God has assigned to us holy guardian angels to protect us. He has given us Scripture to instruct and edify us, and the example of His saints to guide and inspire us. Above all, He provides us with His own true body and blood to nourish our hearts and confirm our strength upon this journey of life.

A sure sign of authentic hope is when a person courageously endures all adversities without complaint and derives encouragement from every good thing which he experiences or perceives. The person who is animated by the virtue of hope will persevere with determination in whatever good works he undertakes, in accordance with the words of the psalm: "Take courage and let your heart be strong, all you who hope in the Lord."[164]

---

[164] Psalms 30:25.

A PRAYER TO GOD FOR HOPE

O Lord, Your promise of perfect beatitude in the kingdom of heaven is the source and object of humanity's hope. By hoping in this promise, our trust and faith in You is expressed, and we are sustained upon the journey of life, to face all the uncertainties and tribulations of this world. By this holy hope our joy is sustained, and our perseverance in good works animated.

Whenever I feel my hope to waver or become dim, may I call to mind what You gave to secure for us the assurance of final blessedness—Your sufferings and death upon the cross, the sacred wounds You bore, and the precious blood which You poured out for our salvation. And not only this, but You have assigned to us guardian angels to protect us on our way, and have given Your very own body and blood to sustain us during this mortal pilgrimage. When I consider such awesome things, my hope shall be made utterly secure and invincible, and will burn with vibrant and joyful expectation of the wonderful things You have promised.

O Lord, may You Yourself be my hope as long as I am on earth, just as You shall be the fulfillment of all my hopes in heaven, who live and reign forever and ever. Amen.

22

HOLY FEAR

Holy and righteous fear is manifested in the diligent observance of the divine precepts, both in actions and in faith. Again, this same wholesome fear is the natural sense of anxiety or hesitation that causes a person to avoid or to shun illicit or sinful activities, both in his exterior actions and in the interior motions of the affections and thoughts. For by such illicit and sinful activities (whether they are done in exterior works or remain simply as internal motions), the soul becomes separated from God, or at least temporarily estranged from His friendship.

The person who is animated and directed by holy fear will be cautious in his use of the things of the senses, lest his mind and affections are drawn away from God by things like food, or drink, or sleep, or by excessive delights in any created thing. This drawing away from God, by the indulgence in the things of the senses, has the effect of causing faith and devotion to become tepid and lukewarm.

A good wife should always be concerned that she does not in any way offend her beloved husband—either through her actions or movements, or words or expressions. In the same way, souls in which holy fear abides will always be concerned that they do not cause God any offense in anything they do. And just as a good wife will be attentive even to minor matters in order to express her devotion to her husband, so the virtuous soul will also be conscious of minor and venial sins which may offend God, even though they may not be of any great importance in themselves. For venial sins, if repeated frequently or habitually, lead to a gradual separation from God, and often pave the way for the more serious estrangement of mortal sin.

We should be encouraged in the cultivation of holy fear by a consideration of the many useful effects of this virtue. It is indeed the beginning of wisdom, as the psalmist testifies: "The beginning of wisdom is the fear of the Lord."[165] It is also the beginning of righteousness, according to the verse: "The one who is without fear of the Lord cannot be made righteous."[166] [As well as being the beginning of righteousness and wisdom,] holy fear may also be considered to be the seal or conclusion of all the other virtues, as is expressed in the verse: "The fear of the Lord places itself

---

[165] Psalms 110:10.
[166] Ecclesiasticus 1:28.

above all other virtues."[167] And where there is not holy fear, all other graces are soon dispersed and dissipated, and conscience and goodness inevitably come to fall away. This is expressed in the verse: "If you do not abide in the fear of the Lord, your whole edifice shall soon be subverted."[168]

Another benefit of holy fear is explained by Saint Bernard, who writes, "In truth, I have learnt that there is nothing so effective in obtaining, retaining, and recuperating grace than to regard God with constant awe, reverence, and fear. 'Blessed is the one who is never without holy fear.'[169] Be filled with reverence and awe then when you discover that a grace has been given to you. Be fearful also when you find that the grace is not there. And be solicitous when you find it has been restored to you. For this is to be 'never without holy fear.'"[170]

A consideration of the fall of so many magnificent angels before the creation of the world ought to fill us with a certain fear and solicitous trepidation, and an awareness that we can never take our final salvation for granted, no matter how virtuous or holy we may be. Speaking of these

---

[167] Ecclesiasticus 25:14.

[168] Ecclesiasticus 27:4.

[169] Proverbs 28:14.

[170] Bernard's meaning is that a person should be filled with a sense of awe and humility when he receives some grace, when he feels a grace to be absent from him, and when he discovers it has been restored. This does not imply fear of the grace itself in any negative sense but a recognition of the unfathomable power of God and a mindfulness of the serious responsibilities attached to spiritual graces.

fallen angels, Job says, "Behold, even those who minister to God are not firmly established [in their merits], and God finds fault even in His angels. How much more so with us, who dwell in fragile vessels of clay and are fashioned out of earth!"[171] In the same way, we can also consider the falling away of many persons who were holy at the beginning, such as Adam, Samson, Solomon, and even all the apostles [except for Saint John], who abandoned Christ at His passion.

And even today, we see a multitude of holy persons falling away from virtue and goodness. There are many who assume that, in the Final Judgment, all will go well for them. But, alas, many are deceived! For they presume to be saved by their own goodness, merits, and efforts, but often these are (sadly) not so great nor so firmly established as they imagine them to be.

The examples of the saints expressing fear of the Lord should inspire us to cultivate this same holy fear. The holy Job expressed such fear when he exclaimed, "Like one whom the waves of the ocean washed over, even thus I feared the Lord."[172] In another place, he says, "All my [feelings and thoughts] seemed to sink into a profound abyss."[173] The commentary in the *Glossa Ordinaria* says of this verse: "Consider—who is there who may rest securely

---

[171] Job 4:18–19.
[172] Job 31:23.
[173] Job 17:16.

and with complete assurance when [even Job] whom the divine Judge praised experiences such trepidation?"

And Saint Jerome, speaking of himself, confessed, "Every time I think of the Day of Judgment, then my whole body trembles with fear!" What trepidation, therefore, should we miserable wretches feel when even such holy men have freely declared themselves to be fearful!

SIGNS OF GENUINE AND COUNTERFEIT FEAR

A sign of genuine fear of the Lord is for a person to be carefully solicitous in all matters pertaining to God so that he never neglects them, in any time or place. Such people will do whatever works of piety and devotion are reasonably possible for them, and will fulfill all their religious and moral obligations with fervor. Hence it is written in the book of Ecclesiastes: "The one who fears God does not neglect any matter."[174] And in Ecclesiasticus, it is likewise written, "The one who fears God shall do good works."[175]

But a sign of counterfeit or insincere fear of the Lord is when a person does good things and avoids sin, not out of love or fear of the Lord, but rather out of consideration of his own self-interest. Such persons are not really motivated

---

[174] Ecclesiastes 7:19.
[175] Ecclesiasticus 15:1.

by fear of God or divine judgment but rather only by fear of losing their own possessions, reputation, or status. The Lord Himself firmly prohibits such types of worldly fears in the Gospel when He admonishes us, "Do not fear those who can kill the body, [but cannot kill the soul]!"[176] And similarly, we read in Isaiah, "Who are you that you should be fearful of any human being?"[177]

A PRAYER TO GOD FOR HOLY FEAR

Lord, grant to me holy fear—for this is the beginning and the end of all wisdom, the solid foundation of true justice, and the guard and protector of all the other virtues. Indeed, unless preserved by holy fear, all the other virtues are soon dissipated and vanished, like dust blown away by the wind.

When I consider the fall of so many angels and the ruin of so many great human beings, let me be filled with trembling and trepidation lest I too should fall away, and preserve me from all complacency. For I am but a fragile and weak mortal, vacillating and vulnerable to temptation. Keep an earnest dread of that tremendous Final Judgment always before the eyes of my heart so that I will flee not only sin but even all the occasions of sin, and everything that may separate me from You. Amen.

---

[176] Matthew 10:28.
[177] Isaiah 51:12.

23

SPIRITUAL JOY

True joy or spiritual delight is to find all of one's consolation in the things of God. Indeed, we find in God the substance and material of all true joy—namely, power, wisdom, goodness, generosity, beauty, mercy, justice, truth, nobility, sanctity, gentleness, faithfulness, charity, humility, and all other admirable and desirable qualities. And these are all to be found in God in complete and utter perfection, and to an infinite and eternal extent.

A person will possess this spiritual joy if he maintains a clear conscience in all his actions, and never knowingly transgresses the divine commandments. Such a person will be always striving to progress in holiness and sanctity, through imitation of the virtues and sanctity of our Lord Jesus Christ, and by perfect conformity to the divine precepts. The apostle [Saint Paul] rejoiced and gloried in this purity of conscience when he declared, "The testimony of our own conscience is founded in simplicity of heart and in the sincerity of God rather than in any wisdom of this world. It assures us that we enjoy the grace of God, even while in this world."[178]

We should be led to this joy by consideration of the wonderful fact that God, who is infinitely good above all else, chose a human nature, out of all His creation, to be united with Him in His glory and beatitude. And the glory and beatitude that God possesses through His divine nature, human beings will also possess through God's saving grace. For He did not choose the angels to be united to Himself, but He chose rather the offspring of Abraham, as the apostle states.[179] Hence Saint John Chrysostom exclaims, "Is it not a truly marvelous thing that our human flesh shall be enthroned in the glory of heaven, and there shall be adored and served by the angels?"

Another potent encouragement to spiritual joy is the fact that God has given His own assurance and promise of this eternal beatitude, guaranteed by the law and the prophets, and even by His own oath. We read this in Luke: "He has sworn that what He promised on oath to our father Abraham, He is to bestow upon us."[180] This promise of eternal beatitude is further confirmed by the four Evangelists, by the apostles, and by the Holy Spirit through the sacrament of Baptism. Moreover, we have evidence of this through

[178] 2 Corinthians 1:12.
[179] Hebrews 2:16.
[180] Luke 1:73.

the spiritual foretastes of the sweetness of heaven [which God sometimes grants to the faithful in contemplation]. And we also have the sacramental presence of the Son of God Himself, our Lord Jesus Christ, as a kind of surety or pledge of this promise.

The apostle [Saint Paul] exhorts us to rejoice in a twofold form. For he writes, "Rejoice in the Lord always (that is, in mystical union with God); and again I say, rejoice! (because of the guarantee of eternal beatitude)."[181]

TRUE AND FALSE JOY

There is abundant material for joy for the Christian soul. For, by an internal inspiration and by the efficacy of the sacraments, God often bestows the grace of complete certainty that all of one's sins have been forgiven. This is even the case when we have offended Him and all of creation by our wrong actions, and lost the graces bestowed upon us. When this has happened, divine forgiveness can fully restore that which has been lost and wipe away the guilt of our misdeeds. Saint Mary Magdalene had this complete certainty of full forgiveness; for the Lord had said to her, "Her many sins are forgiven her, for she has loved much."[182] The same spiritual joy, resulting from complete confidence

---

[181] Philippians 4:4.
[182] Luke 7:47.

in the gracious forgiveness of God, was experienced by Saint Francis of Assisi, of whom it is said: "At last, it was revealed to him internally that all his guilt was remitted."[183]

Further material for joy is the consideration that each human being [through divine grace] is a son or daughter of God. For this reason, we are all heirs, by God's decree, to the kingdom of heaven! The Holy Spirit bestows assurance of this awesome fact, as the apostle [Saint Paul] declares, "The Spirit gives testimony to our spirit, that we are the children of God. And if we are children, then we are heirs, and, indeed, coheirs with Christ."[184] Saint Paul had this joyful certitude when he said, "I am certain that neither death, nor life, nor any created thing, is able to separate us from the love of God!"[185]

But there is also a false joy, which is not truly a virtue at all. This false joy is to be delighted in passing things, or material possessions, or carnal friendships, or physical comfort, or worldly good fortune. All of these joys are unstable and insecure, and are therefore snares for sorrow. For when they pass away (as they inevitably must), then the happiness which they brought will similarly vanish, to be replaced with grief and sadness. And unless the heart is able to free

---

[183] This verse is taken from an antiphon in the Mass for Saint Francis of Assisi.
[184] Romans 8:16–17.
[185] Romans 8:38–39.

itself from the burden of such worldly sorrow, it shall never enter into true spiritual joy. For joy and sorrow are not able to exist simultaneously in the same heart, in the same way that fire and water cannot occupy the same space. For they are in essential conflict, and one expels the other.

A Prayer to God for Spiritual Joy

What great causes we have for joy, O Lord, when we consider the magnificent privileges and graces You have bestowed upon us! And how blessed it is to contemplate Your infinite perfection, in which is found the source of all happiness! For You possess power, wisdom, justice, goodness, beauty, innocence, and mercy, and everything which is worthy of love and admiration, in its ultimate degree.

And shall my soul not be filled with delight to reflect upon the fact that You have chosen the human race out of all Your creatures to be partakers of Your glory and perfection, and have bound Yourself to us in the unbreakable bonds of the Incarnation?

Grant me the wisdom to seek and find my joy in nothing but You, O Lord, rather than in the fleeting and inconstant things of this passing world. Let me rejoice both in the enjoyment of mystical contemplation of Your glory during this life and in the promise of eternal beatitude in the next world. Amen.

24

HOLY SADNESS

There is a certain kind of holy sadness, or compunction, that is regarded as a virtue. This is to feel pain in one's heart for all the multitude of wrongs and injustices that our innocent Lord has sustained. These injustices against God commenced at virtually the beginning of creation [when the evil angels first rebelled], and they will extend until the very end of the age [as long as people continue to sin]. The pain that arises in the heart of one who truly loves the Lord, and who considers deeply all that He has endured and suffered, ought to bring forth innumerable burning tears from his eyes and passionate sighs from the depths of his heart![186]

Another source of this holy sadness or compunction is when a person considers how often he has been overcome

---

[186] This holy sadness of which Albert speaks, arising from feeling pain for the wrongs which God has sustained, obviously reaches its peak in the contemplation of the passion of Christ. This type of sadness should not be understood as being in opposition to, or incompatible with, the joy described in the previous chapter.

by temptation, and has not exercised fitting resistance or fortitude. How often it is that merely seeing or hearing something that is unbecoming or indecent gives rise to a multitude of impure thoughts and disordered feelings! And when the mind perceives any object, action, or word through the five senses which is able to provoke it to vainglory, envy, anger, rancor, detraction, avarice, flippancy, or lust, how very often it is that it immediately falls into such sins without offering any firm or determined resistance.

Then, there are those who, having once fallen into the mire of sinful patterns of thought or actions, never succeed in arising from them. And even if we do manage to free ourselves by means of divine grace, can we be certain that we shall not fall again? We human beings easily fall by our own actions, but, alas, we cannot rise again by our own actions! For we are all weighed down by our mortal flesh, which is fashioned from the very dust of the earth.

Another consideration that is conducive to holy sadness is the realization that we have received many graces and gifts from the infinite font of divine mercy but have failed to employ these adequately and to their full potential. Like the servant who buries the talent entrusted to him, how often do we neglect to use our abilities, opportunities, and graces fully and in accordance with God's plan.[187]

---

[187] See Matthew 25:14–30.

Each of these considerations in themselves ought to be enough to move any human heart to genuine and profound sorrow, and all of creation combined could not shed sufficient tears to mourn worthily even one of them!

The example of Christ Himself serves to affirm for us the spiritual value of holy sadness, for we read that He was often moved to sorrow, and that He frequently shed tears. Indeed, in the beatitudes, He declared, "Blessed are those who mourn, for they shall be comforted."[188] For except by going through sadness, no one is able to arrive at genuine joy.

We should be encouraged to appreciate holy sadness when we consider its great spiritual and moral usefulness. This spiritual and moral usefulness is expressed in the verse from Ecclesiastes: "It is better to go to the house of mourning than the house of rejoicing."[189] For holy sadness is conducive to compassion, kindness, and humility. It can help reduce the power of sensory temptations and make a person more restrained and circumspect in his words and actions.

This contrasts with one of the unfortunate effects that occasionally accompanies joy. For sometimes when a person experiences some period of joy or happiness (even of

---

[188] Matthew 5:5.
[189] Ecclesiastes 7:3.

a purely spiritual kind), he becomes less cautious in his words and actions, and so finds himself slipping into sin.

Another useful fruit of spiritual sadness can be an increase in the sincerity and intensity of prayer. While all forms of prayer are pleasing to God, prayer which is accompanied by tears is particularly precious to Him. According to Saint Bernard, God never fails to hear prayers which are made with tears, for these touch His divine heart most deeply.

SIGNS OF HOLY AND WORLDLY SADNESS

A sign of holy sadness is when the mind of the person affected is not depressed or disturbed by its feelings of sorrow but rather raised up to higher things. A person who experiences this holy sadness will not seek to be freed from it by any external reliefs, comforts, or diversions.

But if a person seeks external relief or diversion from a particular feeling of sadness, or if it causes his mind to become agitated and distraught, it is a sure indication that it is *not* holy sadness at all, but merely some earthly sorrow. This earthly sorrow is that of which Scripture speaks, when it is written: "A sad spirit will dry up the bones"[190]—that is, an excess of sadness which has purely worldly causes makes the virtues become enfeebled. Similarly, Saint James

---

[190] Proverbs 17:22.

writes, "Human wrath [that is, the negative feelings which spring from earthly matters] does not achieve the righteousness of God."[191]

A sign that a person is experiencing a holy form of sadness is when he is inclined to withdraw himself from the pleasures of the flesh, and he does not find his feelings changed by the things of the senses. Very often he will enjoy solitude and find that he does not long for human companionship, nor does he seek any consolation in the company of others.

But a sign of worldly sadness is when a person becomes dejected because of the loss of some temporal thing. Again, the sorrow which results from some affliction, or the loss of a loved one (while natural in itself), is not the same as holy sadness. Such natural sadness is a purely human response, and not a sign of a particular grace. Similarly, if this worldly or natural sorrow becomes excessive or uncontrolled or is permitted to last for too long, it can have a harmful and debilitating effect on devotion, virtue, and the spiritual life in general. Accordingly, we read, "As a moth eats away at clothing and a worm eats away at wood, so melancholy can eat away at the human heart."[192] And in another place it is written, "The spirit is cast down by sadness of the soul."[193]

---

[191] James 1:20.
[192] Proverbs 25:20.
[193] Proverbs 15:13.

A Prayer to God for Holy Sadness

Lord, how shall my heart not be touched with compunction and sorrow when I perceive all the offenses which are committed against You by human beings? For You have given to us everything we possess, including existence itself. But so often we show our ingratitude, abusing Your gifts and turning them against You, the loving Giver.

And who would not be moved to the deepest depth of sorrow, even to the shedding of tears like great drops of blood, when they consider the cruel wounds which You sustained upon the cross, and the divine blood which You poured out for our salvation? Make me, O Lord, to weep with You and for You!

Let me seek no consolation in the vain and passing things of this world. Rather, let my only solace be the hope of that endless glory and ineffable beatitude, which (by Your grace) I shall enjoy for all eternity with You, who live and reign forever and ever. Amen.

25

GRATITUDE

The virtue of gratitude shows itself to be true and perfect when the soul constantly praises and extolls the greatness and splendor of all the gifts of the Lord, with all sincerity and reverence. This virtue of gratitude was exhibited by King David, when he glorified the mandates of the Lord, saying, "I have loved your mandates above gold and topaz."[194] And Solomon extolled God's gift of wisdom with similar exuberance and sincerity when he exclaimed, "The Lord's wisdom transcends and surpasses all precious things, and no desirable treasure is worthy of being compared to it!"[195]

The person who truly possesses the virtue of gratitude will recognize that he is unworthy of the great gifts which God has bestowed upon him. And, insofar as he recognizes his unworthiness, the feeling of gratitude will be increased and purified. It is in accordance with this principle that Saint John Chrysostom said, "O Christ, for all that you have given

---

[194] Psalms 118:127.
[195] Proverbs 8:11.

us, you expect nothing in return—except that we should be saved. And this salvation You grant to us graciously and gratuitously, and so, as we recognize all that we have received from Your hand, we offer You our unbounded thanks!"

We ought to be inspired with true gratitude when we consider the infinite greatness and goodness of the One who bestows such spiritual gifts upon us—namely, God Himself. For the celestial Giver of the gifts we receive is omnipotent, infinitely loving, most blessed, and utterly perfect and incomparable in every possible respect.

As well as the splendor and magnificence of the Giver, we should also consider the immensity and preciousness of the gifts which we receive from Him. For the gifts which we receive from God, both spiritual and material, are not mere trinkets or trivial benefits. Rather, they all partake of the immense and unfathomable goodness of God Himself. [For such gifts include existence itself, life, intelligence, faith, mercy, and the promise of eternal bliss.]

It behooves us also to consider the love with which God bestows His gifts upon us. For the affections of the one who gives contribute much to the value of the gift—something given with love acquires a particular and wonderful value for this very reason. Now, God gives us His gifts in no half-hearted manner, nor with anger, nor in the mercenary hope of receiving something in return. Rather, God gives to us with pure, complete, and unselfish love, out of the immensity of His own divine goodness and limitless generosity.

We should reflect, too, on the superlative benefits which we derive from these gifts which we receive from God. For God confers upon us each of His gifts for no other purpose than that we may gain knowledge of His perfection and love, and come, at last, to enjoy eternal beatitude and glory. We should be mindful of our own unworthiness as recipients of these incalculable and priceless gifts. For nothing we could ever do in our own lives could possibly make us worthy of all that God gives to us.

Finally, we should not overlook the great usefulness of the virtue of gratitude. For our gratitude opens the font of heaven's mercy, and unfailingly moves God to compassion. Conversely, ingratitude causes the fountain of mercy to dry up. It makes the dew of clemency vanish, and the streams of grace cease to flow. The more a soul is filled with gratitude, the more will it receive graces and mercy. In this way, our gratitude for the gifts we have received leads to even more and greater gifts being given to us.[196] This, then, increases the virtue of gratitude even more.

A sign of genuine gratitude is when a person gives thanks to God with all his heart for each of the benefits he has received from Him, however great or small. A grateful person will treat these gifts with reverence, and do his utmost to

---

[196] See Matthew 25:29. "To those who have, even more will be given."

retain them and preserve them in pristine and immaculate condition. For how could a friend be considered truly grateful for a gift if he treated it negligently and carelessly, or soon lost it?

It behooves us not to cultivate gratitude only for those things which bring us comfort and consolation but even for those things which cause us some suffering or affliction. For all of these, both consolations and afflictions, come from one and the same wisdom and goodness of God. Accordingly, Tobit said, "I bless You, Lord God of Israel, for You have castigated me, and, [by means of this,] You have saved me!"[197] God both bestows blessings upon us and permits tribulation to befall us for one and the same purpose—namely, the attainment of grace in this present life, and future glory in the world to come. And very often something which is experienced as an affliction at the time will lead to some more useful outcome in the longer term. Thus Job said, "If we accept good things from the hand of God, must we not also accept evil?"[198] In these words, he is counselling us that we should accept both with gratitude and graciousness.

A sure sign of ingratitude is when a person closes his heart to accepting good spiritual gifts from God. How is the heart closed to receiving these spiritual gifts? By allowing

---

[197] Tobit 11:17.
[198] Job 2:10.

it to be filled with bad will, or rancor, or flippancy, or excessive delight in temporal things, or carnal attachments. For the heart which is filled with such things cannot easily accept the graces which God would confer upon it.

Another indication of ingratitude is when a person does not take due care to preserve the gifts he has received from God, or when he does not make adequate efforts to develop and increase his graces and talents, or when he does not employ them usefully and in accordance with the divine plan.[199] And another, and even more grave, display of ingratitude is when a person misuses the gifts he has received from God (whether powers of mind, body, or soul) to do things which are contrary to His commandments. Alas, this happens all too often! And whoever is so ungrateful as to use the gifts he has received in a manner which is opposed to, or dishonors, the supreme Giver surely deserves to be deprived of them completely!

A PRAYER TO GOD FOR GRATITUDE

O Lord, explain to me, I beg You, just who You are. For You have given me such immense and unimaginable benefits—to me, who have done absolutely nothing to deserve them! And it is not only innumerable graces and benefits You have conferred upon me but Your very self. And I barely deserve

---

[199] See Matthew 25:14–30.

to be counted amongst the very least and most lowly of Your creatures. Is it that Your own glory will be increased if I love You and am thankful to You? Far from it!

Rather, it is Your most pure and overflowing goodness alone which impels You to draw mankind to Yourself, and for You to give Yourself to us. This same infinite goodness leads You to make us sharers in Your own perfect and eternal beatitude, which is Your most perfect gift.

May I recognize that what I receive from Your hand, O Lord—whether it is consolation or affliction, joy or sorrow—is given to me solely to bring me to this final and perfect happiness. May I feel for You always due gratitude, for You have given to me a gift beyond all imagining—Your very self! Amen.

26

ZEAL FOR SOULS

The virtue of "zeal for souls" may be said to be perfect when a person labors for the salvation of souls (both their own and those of others) with all his heart and all his efforts. These labors will be accompanied with holy meditations, fervent desires, tears, prayers, vigils, fasts, and other good works. According to the state of life of the person, it may also include efforts to exhort others in the Gospel, such as preaching, teaching, and the offering of spiritual counsel.

Saint Bede the Venerable speaks of the value of the grace and virtue of zeal for souls, asking, "What could be more sublime and more pleasing to God than the deeds of those who endeavor in their daily activities to convert more and more souls to the love of their Creator, and thus to increase the ranks of those who delight in the eternal joys of heaven?" Similarly, Saint Gregory said, "There is no sacrifice to the Lord which is comparable to zeal for the salvation of souls!"

The example of our Lord Jesus Christ ought to encourage each of us to this holy zeal for souls. For in His own life, He exhibited passionate fervor for the conversion of sinners, for the perfection of the life of the virtuous, and for the recuperation of souls that were otherwise lost. So great was this fervor and zeal which animated Him that, in the end, He gave His own life-blood up in a most horrendous death in order to redeem souls for the kingdom of heaven and to restore them to love of the Father. Saint Bernard testifies that Christ was so ardent in His desire to save others that He disregarded completely the cost to Himself. How immense then was the zeal for souls which burnt within the Sacred Heart of Jesus! It was such that He poured forth His blood in torrents to save each one of us. Yet even one single drop of this most precious blood would have sufficed to redeem the entire human race!

Thus each soul is clearly of an incalculable value to God. The immensity of this value is something wholly beyond our comprehension; yet it was known perfectly to Christ, who is the Wisdom of God. Our failure to grasp and appreciate this great preciousness of our immortal souls is something about which Saint Bernard lamented, saying, "Alas, how little we consider the extraordinary value of our souls while we live in this present life and remain so negligent of the state and condition of our immortal soul. But the preciousness of our souls is easily demonstrated—for we need only consider what becomes of a human body once the soul, the principle of life, has departed from it! God considered our souls to be so important and precious that He gave His only-begotten Son to redeem them for Himself. And even the devil understands the pricelessness of the human soul—for he is willing to offer the entire world to purchase a single one!"

A sign of genuine and commendable zeal is when a person cares more for the winning of souls for Christ then he does about his own personal convenience, or even his life itself. King David exhibited such holy zeal when he cried out, "O my son Absalom, O Absalom my son! How I wish I could have given my life for your salvation!"[200] And the apostle [Saint Paul] similarly wrote, "I would happily give myself, and give more than my own self, for your soul!"[201] Again, he declares, "Each day I die, all for the sake of your glory, brothers and sisters!"[202]—meaning figuratively by this, "Each day I undergo peril of death for the sake of the salvation of your souls."

This virtue of zeal for souls was equally displayed by the great Saint Dominic. Once when he heard of a person who had been kidnapped by Saracens, he wished to offer himself into their custody so that the kidnapped person could

---

[200] 2 Samuel 18:33.
[201] 2 Corinthians 12:15.
[202] 1 Corinthians 15:31.

be released. And the same thing happened with another person who had been kidnapped by heretics. Nevertheless, in both instances, the Wisdom of God intervened and prevented this from happening, thus saving blessed Dominic to undertake his great work for the salvation of innumerable other souls.

A sign of false zeal or counterfeit fervor is when a person applies himself to spiritual duties more for the praise and rewards he will accrue than for saving souls. Sometimes people *appear* to be animated by zeal, but they labor more for gaining the friendship and favor of others than for advancing their sanctification and virtue. Such was definitely not the case for the apostle [Saint Paul], who said, "I do not seek to obtain your favor or your possessions, but your very selves."[203]

It is to be noted, however, that very often persons (even good and holy ones) are motivated by a double motive— namely, God, and something else. And it is difficult to know with accuracy what such motives are, and whether the love of God or some ulterior motive is the principal force at work. For example, a brother may be willing and enthusiastic in hearing confessions. Indeed, he may genuinely wish to save souls for the sake of God, but he may also wish to obtain favor, friendship, diversion, or some other benefit. Such situations are not easy to discern, but

---

[203] 2 Corinthians 12:14.

a good way of judging would be by asking: Is this person more enthusiastic in hearing the confessions of the rich, the noble, the young, and the beautiful than he is in hearing the confessions of the poor, the common, the old, and the homely?

A sure sign of genuine and holy zeal is when a person seeks in his labors to promote the glory of God more than to obtain any benefits or advancements for himself. There are certain types of holy work which require great effort, and yet carry some rewards and satisfactions—such as preaching, hearing confessions, leading a church or a community, et cetera. But, though there are rewards attached to such works, there are also many perils. On the other hand, there are other types of holy works (such as fasting, keeping vigils, and undertaking acts of penance) which bring no personal advancement or worldly rewards, but, on the other hand, contain very few perils or risks. A person motivated by genuine fervor will undertake both types of works with equal eagerness and dedication. On the other hand, a person whose zeal is not genuine will always incline more towards works of the first variety, since they are more visible and more likely to be received with the appreciation and approbation of others.

A PRAYER TO GOD FOR ZEAL FOR SOULS

Lord, mankind certainly does not properly appreciate the immense value of their own souls! Yet You have shown to us how greatly You value our souls—for You descended from the ineffable glory of heaven and underwent death on the cross, all for the sake of gaining our souls for Yourself. If You, O Lord, valued our souls so highly, should I regard them lightly, as things of no consequence? Heaven forbid!

Rather, should I not be fully ready to burn, or to melt, for the sake of the salvation of the souls of others? Shall holy zeal not consume my heart when I see human souls—for which You suffered agony on the cross—perish and be eternally lost?

My Lord and my King, inflame my heart with such holy zeal so that I may be ready both to live and to die for the salvation of my own soul, and those of my brothers and sisters. For in doing this, I shall imitate You, O Jesus, who live and reign forever and ever. Amen.

27

LIBERTY

True liberty may be said to exist when a person is not bound by the chains of sin and vice. For these are what really imprison the soul, as is written, "A wicked person is captured by his iniquities; and bound up by the chains of his sins."[204] And sin is also what makes a person to become like a slave, as Scripture testifies: "All who sin become the slaves of sin."[205]

To commit sin is *not* liberty or freedom (as some people mistakenly imagine), nor is it any part of liberty. Saint Anselm wisely observes that sin is, on the contrary, the very worst form of servitude. For there is no one who is able to liberate himself, or another, from this type of wretched and abject slavery. It cannot be achieved except by the grace of Christ. Accordingly, the Gospel proclaims, "If the Son has set you free, you shall be free indeed."[206]

---

[204] Proverbs 5:22.
[205] John 8:34.
[206] John 8:36.

The person who has attained true freedom will not be held captive by any desire for temporal things. Nor shall he be controlled by the praise or favor of other people, nor by considerations of his own comfort, nor by servile fear, nor by the delight of any transitory joys.

We should be led to the love of true freedom by a consideration of God's divine ordinance and will, which decreed that human beings should be free. As a sign of this intention, God bestowed upon human beings alone free judgment and free will. And it is in this respect that human beings most closely resemble the divinity. For just as God cannot be compelled by any other being, so the will and judgment of a person cannot be coerced by any other. This divine gift of free will and judgment was given to human beings at the beginning of creation, as Ecclesiasticus testifies: "When God created mankind from the beginning, He left them under the control of their own judgment."[207]

A person will infallibly arrive at perfect freedom if he consciously and deliberately binds himself to the inviolable observance of all divine laws and counsels, as well as whatever vows he has committed himself to. A person will achieve spiritual liberty when he has learned to restrain his mind and his senses from all pleasures and temptations of the senses. Freedom comes with learning to love and accept obedience—not with resentment, but with genuine love. The more a person

---

[207] Ecclesiasticus 15:14.

cultivates these things in his heart, the closer he will come to arriving at perfect, holy, and divine liberty.

But those who live in the world in a so-called "libertine" fashion, or who follow the calls and commands of pleasure and pride, do not achieve any true freedom at all. On the contrary, they become enslaved to their own vices, and are soon bound up by the snares of the devil. Ironically, the more "free" and unrestrained they seem to become in their outward behavior, the more they have really become thralls and slaves of their own vile wickedness!

A sign that a person has attained true liberty is when he is constrained by no desires which would separate or distance him from God. But, contrary to this, it is often people who are elevated to positions of authority [and who therefore *seem* to be free] who become most oppressed and enslaved by worldly concerns. They necessarily become entangled in a range of business and are solicitous about other people's affairs. In addition to this, they often find themselves obliged to participate in luxurious dinners and feasting, and also they are frequently compelled to defend their actions and decisions from criticism. Thus the "liberty" apparently enjoyed by persons in authority is often merely illusory.

A sure sign of true freedom is when a person has enough security of mind and self-confidence for him to be able to acknowledge honestly his own sins and failings, and to repent for them without hesitation. When a truly free person is aware that he has committed some sin or incurred some fault, he will immediately strive to remedy whatever has happened. His awareness of his own culpability and failing will burn in his heart like a fire, manifesting itself in fervent prayer and penitence. And through such prayer and penitence, he will promptly wash away the stain of sin from his soul, just as fire cleanses rust from iron.

But a symptom of spiritual servitude or captivity is when a person is unable to accept directions without resentment, and when he flares up in the face of any correction, even if it is charitable and friendly in its nature. A person who does not enjoy inner freedom will find himself constantly bound up with thoughts of revenge and unable to let go of grudges.

A person who is controlled by considerations of gaining the praise and approval of others similarly cannot be said to be truly free, nor can anyone whose main source of delight is gifts, rewards, emoluments, or other tokens of favor. It is a wise proverb which warns us, "To accept a bribe is to sell your freedom."[208] And similarly, we read in the book of Job, "A fire shall devour the tents of those who accept bribes"[209]—that is, the fire of false or mercenary friendship, by which liberty is devoured.

---

[208] It is important to note that the word used to indicate a bribe in Latin (*munus*) is the same as the word for a gift.
[209] Job 15:34.

Solomon, speaking of those who bestow gifts, favors, and bribes upon others, observed, "The one *giving* acquires for himself victory and honor, but the one *receiving* bargains away his very soul!"[210]

The attitudes noted above, [resentment of instruction and correction, and desire for praise and rewards,] all serve to reduce and diminish personal freedom, and if they become dominant, they can reduce an individual to a condition of abject spiritual servitude. Alas, such a person is not able to delight in the true liberty of the Spirit of God—for he will be entirely occupied with the earthly and temporal considerations which constrain his soul and enchain his heart.

A PRAYER TO GOD FOR LIBERTY

O Lord, when You created me You bestowed upon me the immense grace of free will, which is not able to be coerced by anyone or anything. Moreover, You gave Your own precious blood to liberate me from enslavement to sin and thralldom to Satan. You constantly strengthen and reinforce my freedom by Your free grace. And yet, how is it that I so often misuse and abuse this freedom? How is it that sometimes I voluntarily place myself under the control of the forces of evil within me and around me, and allow myself to be enchained by sins and vices? How is it that I

---

[210] Proverbs 22:9.

allow my heart to become so easily entrapped by fleshly temptations and the vain blandishments and delights of this passing world?

O Lord, it seems to me that I am constantly sinning against You by falsely persuading myself that freedom consists in following *my* own will perfectly, and allowing myself to be led about wherever my appetites and desires impel me. But in all of these things, I am simply placing myself into a most miserable form of captivity!

O God, You are my liberator! Grant to me that true freedom which only You can give. Join me to Yourself so that I may accept the sweet yoke of obedience to Your holy will, and grant me to understand that my most sublime liberty consists in complete submission to You, who live and reign forever and ever. Amen.

28

SPIRITUAL LIVING

Genuine religion is to live a life which is spiritual, as Saint James testifies, "True religion is this: to come to the aid of orphans and widows in tribulation, and to keep one's soul unstained by the world."[211] For a person to keep himself unstained by the world means to hold himself aloof from the corrupt and dissipated morality of this wicked age. Spiritual living means consciously to avoid all sin, both of a physical and spiritual nature, insofar as this is possible for a human being.

The great usefulness and benefits of spiritual living should lead us to cultivate it carefully and earnestly. For Scripture tells us that "it is the spirit which gives life; the flesh offers nothing."[212] And again, Saint Paul writes, "Those who live in accordance with the flesh cannot please God."[213]

---

[211] James 1:27.
[212] John 6:64.
[213] Romans 8:8.

Those who wish to cultivate a spiritual mode of life ought to avoid and disdain all those things which indulge or pamper the flesh. For such indulgences of the flesh are in conflict with the health and vigor of the spirit, as Saint Peter testifies [when he says, "Dear friends, I urge you, as foreigners and exiles, to abstain from the desires of the flesh, for such things wage war against the soul"].[214] The person intent upon living spiritually will prefer a certain degree of physical austerity and restraint. Such austerity and restraint conserve the graces which have been given by God in much the same way that thorns on plants protect their precious fruits and flowers. For grace can easily flow away or be dissipated through the openings of the mouth, the eyes, and the ears! And just as fire and water cannot exist simultaneously in the same place and at the same time, even so (as Saint Bernard testifies) spiritual and physical pleasure cannot coexist in the same heart at the same time.

Again, we ought to consider that a human being is not able to do any good of himself without the grace of God. The apostle Saint Paul expresses this when he says, "We are not able to claim anything for ourselves, as if it were really our own, but whatever we achieve is from God."[215] Meditation upon this fact should be sufficient to expel all proud

---

[214] 1 Peter 2:11.
[215] 2 Corinthians 3:5.

presumption from our hearts. Nevertheless, we *are* able to do all that is required of us through Christ Himself—and whatever we achieve through Christ will be greater and more perfect than anything we could have done through ourselves. Again, Saint Paul testifies to this when he writes, "We are able to do all things through the One who strengthens us."[216] Just as the former thought should remove all presumption from our hearts, so this latter thought should dispel all despair. For these two—presumption and despair—are both foes of our spiritual well-being. And very often, they fight amongst themselves [to the great detriment and confusion of the soul].

Another consideration which is helpful in spiritual living is the constant, honest recognition of our own faults and failings, and not only our *actual* faults and failings, but also our *potential* ones, if God were not helping us. This should remove any inclinations to pride we might have. And similarly, we should remember that God will demand an account not only for the sins we have committed but also for the good we have failed to do and the graces which we have neglected to use to their full potential. This sober realization should be sufficient to generate a wholesome trepidation in the heart of anyone!

Furthermore, acknowledging that all the good we find in ourselves is God's gift to us should inspire deep

---

[216] Philippians 4:13.

gratitude in our hearts, just as recognizing that the weaknesses which we bear are the result of God's permitting them to arise in us should lead us to accept them with patience and humility. All of these considerations are conducive to leading a life which is more spiritual—that is, a life which is more focused upon God and the soul than on the world and the flesh.

A sign that a person has truly achieved a spiritual mode of living is when the spirit is able to rule and govern all the urges and movements of the flesh. A person who is spiritual will sense any afflictions of the soul and of the conscience just as readily (or, indeed, more readily) than he will notice discomforts of the body. And he will avoid all places, times, and situations which give rise to temptations or spiritual perturbations in just the same way one would avoid whatever causes harm or injury to the body. And when he does suffer some spiritual harm, he will treat it promptly and diligently, just as one would attend to a physical wound. Indeed, since the spirit is higher and more noble than the flesh, so much so should it be treated with even more diligent care and attention!

Another sign that a person's life has become spiritual in its orientation is when an individual takes as much (or more) delight in spiritual nourishment as he does in physical nourishment. A spiritual person will not neglect or omit those activities and observances which provide nourishment and sustenance for the soul any more than a fleshly person would neglect to take his meals!

An indication that a person has not achieved a spiritual manner of life is when he still lives according to the flesh. To "live according to the flesh" means, as Saint Augustine expresses it, "to live according to one's own self or ego." Thus a person may be said to be living according to the flesh if he does whatever his natural impulses prompt him to do. For example, he will sleep whenever, wherever, and for however long he feels like. He will eat and drink whatever he likes and as much as he likes, and whenever he feels like it. An unspiritual person, living according to the flesh, laughs and jokes without prudence and restraint, whenever and with whomever he wishes. Whatever delights the nostrils, he seeks to smell; whatever is gratifying to the touch, or pleasing to the eyes, or delightful to the taste, he pursues eagerly—regardless of whether these things are licit or illicit to him. Alas, beautiful clothing and rich apparel, as well as fine horses and splendid arms, lure and attract him much more than anything pertaining to God or religion!

Another typical sign of a life which is unspiritual and lived according to the impulses of the flesh is a lack of restraint of the tongue. This lack of control of speech is normally a symptom of a distracted and divided heart, just as the apostle Saint James observes, "If anyone thinks himself to be religious, but cannot restrain his tongue, then his religion is in vain."[217] Similarly, it is written, "The one who can restrain his mouth and keep his tongue under control guards his soul from many anxieties."[218] And in another place, we read, "Life and death lie in the control of the tongue."[219]

A PRAYER TO GOD FOR A SPIRITUAL MANNER OF LIVING

O Lord, pour out into me Your Spirit so that I may become entirely Yours and live a life which is truly spiritual. Make me realize that of myself alone, I can do nothing—and through this consideration, let all proud presumption be expelled from my soul. But make me also realize that with You I can do anything—and by this realization, let all discouragement and despondency be removed from me.

Grant that my spirit and my intellect may be able to govern and control the impulses and actions of my body. May I learn to love restraint, simplicity, and austerity in all matters of physical living so that my spirit may grow stronger and more pure. Insofar as my soul is more noble than my

---

[217] James 1:26.
[218] Proverbs 21:23.
[219] Proverbs 18:21.

flesh, let my chief concern and care be the health of my soul rather than that of my body!

Let me always strive to be united with You, O Lord, and to enjoy this wonderful mystical union, and for the sake of this great grace, let me shun all that could separate me from intimacy with You or estrange me from Your friendship. Amen.

29

GRAVITY[220]

True gravity has been attained only when all the affections and powers of the soul are directed unanimously towards God. When this state has been achieved, the mind is restrained from all vanity, and the five senses are no longer distracted and dissipated by external temptations. But when a soul recedes from this blessed condition of gravity, it will very often immediately fall back into the innumerable vanities of this earthly life. For, as we read in the book of Ecclesiastes, "All things under the sun are vain."[221]

---

[220] In the Latin text, the term Albert uses is *maturitas*, which could be literally translated as "maturity." However, Albert uses as the term as a synonym for a prevailing seriousness and restrained dignity of character, which seems to be best designated by the English expression "gravity." This virtue of gravity should not be understood as entirely precluding humor or levity when the occasion requires it. It is important to note, however, that during most of the Middle Ages, loud laughter was generally regarded as a sign of a morally or mentally defective character.
[221] Ecclesiastes 1:14.

The most holy example of our Lord Jesus Christ should encourage us in the pursuit of this perfect gravity. Concerning the seriousness of Christ, Saint Augustine wrote, "We read in the Gospels that our Lord Jesus felt sorrow, that He mourned, that He suffered from fatigue, and sustained injuries, insults, spittle, scourging, and the pain of the cross. But we *never* read that He laughed, nor that He enjoyed worldly prosperity. All the elect should find consolation from this example whenever they are oppressed or discouraged by the trials and adversities of this world. And they should not be deceived or distracted by the attractions of the passing and insubstantial pleasures of this life but rather always be mindful that another, and more real, life will follow—that is, the eternal life of heaven."

Similarly, Scripture often reproves and condemns flippancy and imprudent laughter. For example, we read, "I considered laughter to be an error, and to merriment, I said, 'Why do you seek to deceive us?'"[222] In another place, it is observed that "laughter is often mixed with pain, and in the elation of joy there are tears."[223] And the psalmist says to the Lord, "You disapprove of those given to flippant vanities."[224] But most important of all in this context is the grave admonition articulated by Jesus Christ Himself, who

---

[222] Ecclesiastes 2:2.
[223] Proverbs 14:13.
[224] Psalms 30:7.

warns us, "Woe to you who laugh now, for you shall weep and mourn!"[225]

Excessive merry-making and jocularity can distract the mind from intimacy with God, and can also close the heart to receiving His grace.

A sign that a person has attained to true gravity is if he is fully "collected" in his manner and actions, and given neither to idle words nor unbecoming and superfluous gestures, and does not exhibit a dissolute posture or bearing. Neither will he create occasions for levity in others. Rather, a person who possesses the virtue of gravity will be perfectly self-contained, and will regard with disdain all inane distractions and vain trivialities. He will avoid places, company, and occasions where such things are likely to predominate, knowing that (as Scripture testifies), "the one who touches tar will be defiled by it."[226] Similarly, whoever consorts with dissolute people will inevitably be tainted with dissolution himself.

Thus it was with blessed Job, who exemplifies the virtue of noble gravity. Such was his seriousness and dignity that people who were given to inanities and flippant levity even fled from his company, as he attests, "When youths saw me, they hid themselves from my presence."[227] Indeed, so con-

---

[225] Luke 6:25.
[226] Ecclesiasticus 13:1.
[227] Job 29:8.

stant and consistent was his habit of gravity that whenever he departed from it, other people could hardly believe it. For he says, "If I ever laughed or made a joke, they did not believe it—and so the sight of my smile was regarded as a rare and precious thing to them."[228]

A sure sign of levity and a lack of the virtue of gravity is when a person is prone to laughing at others and constantly making jokes (or trying to make them!). A dissolute mode of living, and the habit of associating with those who are given to dissolution, also betoken a deficiency in gravity and personal dignity.

Indeed, persons who are given to undue flippancy and inane levity will even shun the company of people who *are* blessed with dignity and gravity—imagining that this seriousness will somehow damage their health or diminish their vitality. Such an attitude is portrayed in the book of Ecclesiastes, where the writer says [speaking with instructive irony], "Rejoice, O youth, in your youthfulness, and give your heart over to seeking pleasure while you are young! Walk in whatever paths your desires impel you, and follow whatever pleases your eyes!" But then, [speaking more seriously,] he adds, "Remember that for all of these, God shall bring you to judgment."[229]

---

[228] Job 29:24.
[229] Ecclesiastes 11:9.

A PRAYER TO GOD FOR GRAVITY

O Lord, let all the senses, affections, and faculties of my soul be properly collected and focused so that they are not dispersed and divided by the multitude of vanities and distractions in this world.

Whenever I encounter any adversity, pain, or sorrow, such that I am led to shed tears, may I be mindful of Your own example, for the Gospels frequently relate You to have wept, but never record that You laughed. I shall surely be effectively consoled by knowing that in my own tears of grief and pain, I am spiritually united to You, O Lord.

And let the doors of my senses be firmly and judiciously guarded so that nothing inane or vacuous may enter my heart. Rather, let them be open only to You and to that which is holy so that I may partake in and reflect Your own perfect dignity and stability. Amen.

30

SIMPLICITY

True and perfect simplicity consists in not bearing any negative thoughts or ill-will towards any person whatsoever, and not causing harm to anyone. It is for this splendid virtue that Job was first commended, when we read, "There was a man in the land of Uz, Job by name, who was simple and just."[230] The placement of this commendation of Job's simplicity at the beginning indicates that it exceeds all other virtues.

Our Lord exhorted His apostles to the cultivation of simplicity as He sent them forth into the world, counseling them to "be as prudent as serpents, yet as simple as doves."[231] Here, the virtues of prudence and simplicity are conjoined. And these two virtues must always be paired together, lest they lose their character as virtues and turn

---

[230] Job 1:1. This translation follows the Vulgate text, which describes Job as "*simplex et rectus.*" Most modern translations offer a different reading.
[231] Matthew 10:16.

into vices instead. For prudence, if not founded on simplicity, becomes cunning, and simplicity, if not enriched with prudence, becomes mere stupidity or naivety. A dove, a bird which exemplifies the virtue of simplicity, hurts no one, with either its beak or its claws. In the same way, the person of true holy simplicity will harm none, either by his words or by his deeds.

If a person really loves simplicity, he will not permit himself to be occupied by a multitude of earthly concerns. An example of the error of being occupied with many things is given to us in Martha. For wherever there is a multiplicity of concerns, there is complexity of character [which is antithetical to simplicity]. Simplicity arises from seeking one thing alone—the "one thing necessary"[232] of which our Lord speaks. He praises Mary for her attention to this one thing necessary and declares that she has chosen "the better part, which shall not be taken away from her."[233] This "one thing" to be sought is the Supreme Good, in which all other good things are contained. It is indeed the eternal and limitless Good, which is God Himself.

We should be encouraged in the pursuit of simplicity by the great usefulness and benefits which it confers on those who possess it. Scripture tells us that "the word of the Lord

---

[232] Luke 10:42.
[233] Luke 10:42.

is addressed to the simple."[234] For the Lord is indeed on intimate terms with those whose hearts are simple, and it is to the simple that He deigns to reveal the secrets and mysteries of His divinity and glory. Thus Christ reproved the apostles when they were preventing young children from approaching Him, saying to them, "Let the little children come unto Me. For it is to such as these that the kingdom of heaven belongs."[235]

Simplicity is a virtue without which salvation is not possible. For the Lord Jesus warns us that "unless you become like these little ones, you shall never enter the kingdom of heaven."[236] He does not say "become little ones" but rather "become *like* these little ones." By this, He means, "strive to become simple and innocent, like little children."

There is another particular benefit conferred by simplicity. Of this we read in the book of Proverbs, "The one who walks simply, also walks confidently."[237] For the most secure and safe way to approach the kingdom of heaven is the way of simplicity. For it is written elsewhere: "[God] protects those who walk in simplicity."[238]

An indication of genuine and unfeigned simplicity is when a person does not hastily mistrust the words or deeds

---

[234] See Proverbs 3:32.
[235] Matthew 19:14.
[236] Matthew 18:3.
[237] Proverbs 10:9.
[238] Proverbs 2:7.

of others but always assumes the good of his brothers and sisters, and extends to their actions and words a presumption of innocence. A person who possesses the virtue of simplicity will not disparage or detract from the good of others, and will sincerely desire the well-being and salvation of all. He will not wish harm or evil to anyone, and will perform for others whatever good works he can. A simple person will be conscious of the supreme goodness of God, and shall see Him in his innocence of heart. Filled with confidence and trusting in God's goodness, he will submit his will entirely to His, and carefully observe all His commandments.

[But all forms of duplicity are contrary to the virtue of simplicity.] A sign of such duplicity is when a person has one thing in his mouth and another in his heart, and yet another in his actions. An example of this duplicity may be found in the character of Joab, who killed his cousin Amasa. For he held him affectionately by the beard, and said to him, "Greetings, my brother!" But meanwhile, he secretly removed his sword from its sheath and stabbed him to death![239] Contrary to such duplicity, the Lord Jesus said, "Let your word be 'yes' if you mean 'yes'; and 'no' if you mean 'no.'"[240] In other words, whatever you have in your heart, express honestly by your words, and fulfill it with your actions.

---

[239] See 2 Samuel 20:8–10.
[240] Matthew 5:37.

Similarly, blessed James writes, "A double-minded person is inconstant in all his ways."[241] And the Lord clearly condemns such double-minded people—that is, those who seek to serve both God and the devil, or to be occupied in good works and sin at the same time. Accordingly, He says, "No one can serve two masters!"[242] For virtue and vice, and good and evil are by their nature contraries and therefore cannot coexist. And the apostle James describes the impossibility of serving both God and the world when he writes, "Whoever wishes to be a friend of this world becomes the enemy of God."[243]

A sign of false or counterfeit simplicity is when a person strives to exhibit himself as being simple and straightforward in his words and exterior demeanor, and yet his heart is nourishing thoughts which are deceptive and duplicitous, and quite contrary to his own words and the countenance he displays. It is of such persons that the prophet Jeremiah was speaking when he laments, "Let each one guard himself from his neighbor, and place no trust, even in his own brother! For brother overthrows brother, and friends defraud friends."[244]

---

[241] James 1:8.
[242] Matthew 6:24.
[243] James 4:4.
[244] Jeremiah 9:4.

A PRAYER TO GOD FOR SIMPLICITY

O God, You sincerely love those who are simple of heart, and You communicate to them the treasures of Your secret wisdom. Bestow upon me, I implore You, that dove-like simplicity, together with a serpent-like prudence, which You commended to Your disciples. Fleeing from the multitudinous concerns of secular life, may I endeavor to "choose the better part" and to focus my attention on that "one thing necessary." This "one thing necessary" is indeed You alone, O Lord! For in You is to be found the perfection and totality of all other good things.

May I love Your law and Your precepts, and rejoice sincerely in all the good things enjoyed by my neighbors. In true innocence of heart, may I always think well of others. Let my actions accord with my words, and let my words accord with my heart. When I mean "yes," let me say "yes," and when I mean "no," let me say "no," fleeing from all duplicity and shunning all double-mindedness. Grant me the grace, O Lord, to emulate Your own perfect and immortal simplicity. Amen.

31

HOLY SILENCE

The virtue of holy silence has reached its perfection when a person not only restrains the tongue from saying what is profane, wicked, and prohibited (such as detraction, falsehood, perjury, immodesty, flippancy, gossip, grumbling, etc.) but even, at times, from what is permissible and acceptable to say. This restraint is spoken of by the psalmist, where he declares, "I was silent, and refrained even from saying good things."[245] The *Glossa Ordinaria* explains that this line shows that if a person is able to refrain from saying things which are perfectly permissible, then he will certainly not fall into the trap of saying what is forbidden. For indeed, even in apparently harmless speech, our spiritual focus and energies can be dissipated if it is indulged in without measure or control.

How rare is the virtue of restraint of the tongue! Of this, the apostle Saint James testifies when he writes, "All beasts,

---

[245] Psalms 38:3.

birds, serpents and other creatures can be tamed, but no person can govern the tongue! For the tongue is restless, and carries a lethal venom."[246] The commentary in the *Glossa Ordinaria* explains that this indicates that an ungoverned tongue can exceed the wild beasts in ferocity, or the birds of the air in flippancy and caprice, or venomous serpents in its malice and virulence. Those who "sharpen their tongues"[247] to inflict emotional wounds upon others are truly like wild beasts; those who constantly chatter to no purpose are like noisy jackdaws which never cease to squawk; and those who whisper maliciously and share scandalous gossip are like baleful, poisonous serpents who strike in secret. It is of persons of this last type that the psalmist speaks when he says, "The venom of the asp lurks under their tongues!"[248]

We should be led to a love of holy silence by the example of our Lord Jesus Christ Himself. For by His own actions, He commended quietness to us. When He was interrogated concerning the various accusations raised against Him, He chose not to reply, nor to excuse Himself—even though He knew well that the penalty of a most cruel death awaited Him.

Another striking example which should inspire us with an esteem of silence is the case of a certain holy hermit who is said to have retained a pebble in his mouth for some

---

[246] James 3:7–8.
[247] Psalms 63:4.
[248] Psalms 13:3.

three years in order to teach himself the discipline of restraint of speech.[249] Truly, it is much easier to learn to speak than it is to master the art of keeping silence! Hence the wise proverb counsels us that "whoever wishes to learn to speak well, should first learn to keep silence."

A consideration of the great usefulness of judicious and holy silence should also encourage us to cultivate this virtue. For silence has the effect of causing the heart to become collected and settled. It is conducive to tranquility of mind and calmness of conscience. Most importantly, it makes the soul receptive to divine grace.

But, on the contrary, when a person is incapable of keeping a wise silence, he will inevitably find himself encountering many difficulties and troubles, which could otherwise have easily been avoided. Thus it is written, "The person who cannot control his tongue or keep his thoughts to himself is just like an open and exposed city, unguarded and unprotected by any walls."[250]

And where the ability to maintain judicious silence has not been developed, then spiritual perfection has not yet been attained. For we read that "whoever can avoid

---

[249] This curious incident is recounted in the stories of the Desert Fathers concerning a certain Saint Agathon. It is also related that the ancient Greek orator Demosthenes kept a pebble in his mouth for a certain number of years—but he did this not in order to learn silence but to strengthen his vocal articulation.

[250] Proverbs 25:28.

committing any slip or offense with his tongue has attained to perfection."[251] In other words, according to the commentary in the *Glossa Ordinaria*, whoever *cannot* avoid committing any indiscretion with his speech has not reached perfection. And whoever possesses firm discipline over his speech, will also enjoy blessedness, as we read: "Blessed is the one who makes no slip with his tongue."[252]

Signs of Holy and Deficient Silence

A sign of the successful cultivation of this virtue of holy silence is when a person is willing and able to restrain himself from speaking, even on occasions when it is perfectly permissible and appropriate to speak. Indeed, the person who possesses this virtue of silence will sometimes choose not to speak, even though his words would be eagerly welcomed and highly esteemed. Saint Gregory the Great recognizes this sign of virtue in the prophet Isaiah when he observes, "If the prophet Isaiah, who was sent by God to address the people, chose to remain in seven days of silent meditation before daring to speak, how much more should we restrain our speech? For often we are quick to speak, even when there is no necessity or cogent reason for us to do so." Reflecting this same sentiment, we read in the Gospel our

---

[251] James 3:2.
[252] Ecclesiasticus 14:1.

Lord giving us the sobering admonition, "I say to you, on Judgment Day each person will be required to render an account for whatever idle words they have uttered."[253]

An indication of a deficiency in this virtue is when a person is apt to speak so frequently or so assertively that he always stand out in company. Another sign is the offering of comments and observations at inappropriate times (even if the words are edifying, and would be appropriate at another time). Scripture warns us against this tendency when it says, "The wise person will keep silence until an opportune time for speaking arises, but those who are imprudent and undisciplined will not be able to wait to pour forth their words."[254] Yet another sign that a person needs to develop the virtue of silence is when he is prone to speak even though no one is listening to him, and when no one cares to listen to him. Scripture warns us against this futile tendency when it counsels, "Where there is no one to listen, do not pour forth your speech."[255] Another symptom of a lack of discipline in speech is when a person is quick to answer or reply, even before the other person has finished what he is saying. Similarly, to presume to answer questions on behalf of others is an indication of excessive and imprudent loquacity.

---

[253] Matthew 12:36.
[254] Ecclesiasticus 20:7.
[255] Ecclesiasticus 32:6.

Against this practice, we are warned, "O youth, speak only for yourself, and only as much as is necessary!"[256]

An indication of a false or counterfeit love of silence is when a person does not speak, not out of humility or self-restraint, but because he is afraid of appearing foolish or being contradicted or challenged. Or again, to keep silent purely for the sake of gaining praise and approval from others is not a manifestation of this virtue in its authentic and perfect form. Some people use silence to conceal their ignorance, or to appear wise, in accordance with the popular saying: "If a fool keeps silence, he is considered wise."[257] But this practice [though it is often effective and prudent,] cannot be identified with the genuine and sincere cultivation of the virtue of holy silence.

A Prayer to God for the Virtue of Holy Silence

O Lord, place a guard upon my lips so that I may not only refrain from pointless and foolish speech but also so I may see what is useful and good with moderation and control.

Lord, I know that the tongue is as difficult to control as an untamed beast, and that it has the potential to carry the venom of a serpent! Therefore I beg You to grant me the

---

[256] Ecclesiasticus 32:10.
[257] Proverbs 17:28.

grace to restrain myself, and to quietly rest in You alone. Let me learn to love and imitate that silence which You exhibited in the face of those who persecuted and interrogated You. For You stood before those who calumniated and defamed You without striving to excuse Yourself—like a silent lamb before its shearers, even thus You remained!

When it is necessary for me speak, let me carefully observe all rules of courtesy, restraint, and moderation. May every word I say be pleasing to You, O Lord, and never harmful to my soul nor the source of scandal to my neighbor. Amen.

32

SOLITUDE

True solitude is the practice of withdrawing the mind from all exterior occupations and cares, and from all delights in created things. The person who practices this type of spiritual solitude will then direct all his affections, thoughts, and desires towards God alone, to the extent that he thereby becomes one in spirit with God.

The prophet Isaiah exhorts us to this when he [speaking figuratively] says, "Enter into the rock, and hide yourselves within a pit in the earth."[258] To "enter into the rock" is to become immersed in the contemplation of the divinity of Christ. To "hide oneself in the pit of the earth" is to be taken into the sacred wounds of His humanity. The person who conceals himself within the spiritual rock of Christ partakes of genuine and holy solitude. Everyone else is, to some extent or other, still in the midst of the multitude and still distracted. In perfect spiritual solitude, such grace and

---

[258] Isaiah 2:10.

illumination of mind is received, that all desire to see, hear, or think of other things is overcome.

Thus it was that when Moses remained alone on the mountain in the presence of God for some forty days and forty nights, he was so illuminated that such radiance emanated from his countenance that it shone with all the clarity and brilliance of the sun. And the people of Israel were unable to look upon him until he had covered his face with a veil.[259]

We should be encouraged in our love of solitude by the example of our Lord Jesus Christ. Even though He, as the Son of God, could never be truly distracted from the contemplation of the Divinity (for He was Himself that Divinity), nevertheless, He did frequently flee from the crowds. He would then seek out deserted places in order to pray and meditate. And Christ would also separate Himself even from His dearest disciples in order to be alone in prayer. As Luke recounts, during the anxious time preceding His passion, He went forth from them in the garden of Gethsemane, for the distance of a stone's throw.[260] In doing this, Christ shows us that even the holiest persons cannot devote themselves entirely to the contemplation of God while in the company of others.

The same truth is conveyed in the incident of Zacchaeus. For as long as he was still in the midst of the crowd, he could

---

[259] See Exodus 34:33–35.
[260] See Luke 22:41.

not gain a clear view of Jesus. It was only when he had separated himself from the others, and climbed a tree by himself,
that he was able to see the Savior and to hear His words.[261]

In the book of the prophet Hosea, we hear the Lord
speaking of His beloved spouse [that is, of the human soul]
and saying, "I will lead her into the solitude, and there
I will speak to her heart."[262] These words ought to incite
within us a loving desire for this solitude. How blessed is
the soul which hears this invitation of the Lord! For God
speaks these gentle words to the heart, and by them confers
firm confidence, security, and perseverance to the mind.

The example of the ancient Desert Fathers and holy hermits are also an encouragement to the cultivation of solitude. For these saints lived in deserts, mountains, and caves
in order that they might give themselves fully to contemplation of divine realities. We even read, in some cases, of
hermits who did not see, or were not seen by, other people
for some forty years or more.

Signs of Holy and False Solitude

A sign of a holy love of solitude is always to prefer to spend
time with God than anyone or anything else—to prefer the
company of the Creator than that of any created being or

---

[261] See Luke 19:1–10.
[262] Hosea 2:14.

thing. A wonderful example of this may be found in Saint Mary Magdalene. For after the death of Christ, she remained near the tomb, much preferring to gaze upon His resting place than to consort with others. And she longed for Jesus with such ardent desire that she wished to see nothing else but Him. Thus it was that after the ascension of the Lord, when Mary Magdalene (together with Martha and Lazarus) had gone forth into France, she soon chose for herself the contemplative life of a hermit. And thus she lived for thirty years in strict solitude in a mountain cave in prayer and mystical vision. During that time, she consumed no material food or drink, but the holy angels visited her every hour and sustained her physical body with spiritual nourishment alone.[263]

A form of false solitude is when a person is physically alone, but his soul is still occupied with worldly concerns, and an inner discourse continues in his mind, just as if he were in the company of others.

These last two virtues—the cultivation of holy silence and solitude—both lead the mind to the wonderful grace of contemplation. Hence it is written in the Lamentations, "He will sit alone and remain silent; and He shall raise Himself above me."[264]

---

[263] The story that Mary Magdalene lived as a hermit in France for thirty years is based on medieval traditions.

[264] Lamentation 3:28.

A Prayer to God for Love of Solitude

How blessed and happy is the person who dwells with You alone, O God, separated from all others! But how wretched is the person who is separated from You, even though he might be surrounded by the company of a multitude of other people, and be immersed in the tumult of created things!

You grant great peace and tranquility to those who abide with You in holy solitude, and You illuminate them with the radiant light of Your heavenly splendor. For this reason, a countless multitude of the saints have fled human company and sought to live as hermits, with You, O Lord, as their sole companion.

O Divine Spirit, gather my own wandering spirit to You, and let it not be distracted and scattered by the attractions and diversions of the created world. Teach me to be content with Your companionship alone, and to rest happily and securely in Your love. For by doing this, I will draw from You the ineffable sweetness of celestial contemplation in which my highest joy most surely abides. Amen.

33

CONTEMPLATION

Thrue and perfect contemplation is the focusing of all the affections and powers of the mind towards knowing the divine nature. Such contemplation is accompanied by a sensation of delight and wonder. The various aspects of the divine nature which may form the entrance point for contemplation are many, including God's power, wisdom, goodness, love, nobility, generosity, et cetera, as well as the hidden judgments of God, His most holy will, or any other perfection which leads towards God.

The patriarchs, prophets, and holy apostles all experienced this form of contemplation. For the patriarchs and prophets had the hidden judgments of God revealed to them in contemplation through the action of the Holy Spirit. Examples of the fruits of such contemplation include the revelation of the flood to Noah, the revelation of the destruction of Sodom to Abraham, and the foreseeing of the Babylonian exile and captivity of the people of Israel to Jeremiah. Daniel also received his prophetic illumination of the meanings of King Nebuchadnezzar's dreams through contemplation. Such revelations to persons who cultivate contemplation has been the practice of God throughout the ages, as we find written in the book of Amos: "The Lord God does not formulate an oracle, unless he reveals His secret to His servants, the prophets."[265]

God likewise revealed His will to the apostles through His only-begotten Son and expressed to them (through the Son) all His divine perfections. Christ Himself testified to this when He said, "All that my Father has revealed to me, I have made known to you"[266]—so that the apostles could then, in turn, communicate it to future generations (which, indeed, they faithfully did). For, as we read in the psalm, "Their message goes through all the world, and their words to the ends of the earth."[267] But amongst all the apostles, the Lord revealed to the Evangelist Saint John and to Saint Paul His highest and most secret mysteries, for these two were particularly blessed with the virtue of sublime and ecstatic contemplation.

It is to be noted that contemplation, meditation, and cogitation differ from each other. Cogitation is a kind of wandering about of the mind; meditation is mental investigation or analysis; and contemplation is pure

---

[265] Amos 3:7.
[266] John 15:15.
[267] Psalms 18:5.

admiration or wonder. Cogitation, or wandering of the mind, involves no labor, and produces no fruit. Meditation demands effort, and does produce fruit. Contemplation requires no labor or effort, but produces the greatest fruit.

THREE STEPS OF CONTEMPLATION

We may be helped in our pursuit of contemplation by awareness of the three steps involved in it, which Saint Gregory the Great describes. The first step is that the mind should collect itself. The second step is that, having been fully collected, it should begin to perceive itself clearly. The third step is that the soul should ascend above itself and submit itself entirely to God by contemplating its own invisible Creator.

The soul will not be able to succeed in the first step (of collecting itself), unless it can free itself from all images of earthly, and even celestial, things. Whatever intrudes upon the senses—either through vision, hearing, smell, touch, or taste—must be rejected and refused. In this way, the soul can seek its own self in a purely interior manner, and behold itself without the distractions of the outside world. For whenever we permit our minds to become occupied with the things of the senses, our interior being is invaded by a multitude of images and shadows. But when these images and shadows are dispelled, the soul can gaze upon itself and see itself as an incorporeal reality created by God, more exalted than any physical thing. For the soul is animated by God so that it in turn may animate and govern the lower realities of the material world.

The ineffable sweetness and delight of the experience of contemplation ought to induce us to pursue it with eagerness. For the perfect admiration and wonder of the Divinity, in which contemplation subsists, is the starting point for all beatitude and bliss. Truly, the font of all bliss is God Himself. Through contemplation, God becomes mystically known with the eyes of the heart. Then:

> Because He is loved, He is desired;
> Because He is desired, He is sought;
> Because He is sought, He is found;
> Because He is found, He is possessed in perfect
>   union.

This perfect union with God, once it has been acquired and experienced, can never be lost. Concerning this, Saint Bernard wrote, "The soul which has learnt to enter perfectly into itself and to experience the presence of God within its own depths, and to seek there His face continually, could never be tempted or compelled by anything else—not even by the fires of Gehenna, much less by any earthly allurement—to separate itself from this consummate spiritual sweetness. Rather, the pleasures of the flesh and the world will seem no longer to be temptations at all but rather burdens, in accordance with what is said in the book of Ecclesiastes: 'The eye is not satisfied by seeing, nor is the ear by hearing.'"[268]

Hear, O reader, the words of a person who has experienced this spiritual delight: "You are good, O Lord, to those hoping in You and to the souls which seek You."[269] If any soul should ever willingly permit itself to be separated from the ineffable sweetness of pure contemplation once it has achieved it—well, it would be just as bad as being cast out from paradise, or rejected from the gates of heavenly glory!

Hear, now, another expression of the indescribable joy of contemplation from one who had experienced it [namely, King David, the author of the psalms]. He writes, "To you my heart has spoken, 'My face has delighted You!' I shall seek, O Lord, Your face."[270] Hence he writes, "It is good for me to cling to God."[271] He is addressing his own soul when he urges, "Be converted, my soul, in your rest! For the Lord has done wondrous things for you."[272]

---

[268] Ecclesiastes 1:8.
[269] Lamentations 3:25.
[270] Psalms 26:8.
[271] Psalms 72:28.
[272] Psalms 114:7.

I say, therefore, that the person who has once experienced the celestial delight of the contemplation of God will fear nothing so much as the loss of this grace, and to be forced to enter once again into the consolations (or rather desolations!) of the flesh. Saint Augustine certainly experienced this contemplation. Hence it is that he wrote, "Everything which I ever did in the world somehow displeased me, and seemed to me to be a burden. No longer was I inflamed by fleshly desires, nor ambitions of wealth or honor, as I had been previously. I found that nothing delighted me any longer, O Lord, except Your own sweetness and the beauty of Your dwelling place, which I had come to love so ardently!"

SIGNS OF TRUE AND FALSE CONTEMPLATION

A reliable indication of the strong presence of the virtue of contemplation is when a person feels a certain detachment from, and even weariness with, the things of this passing world. Thus it was that Tobit declared, "It would profit me more to die than to live!"[273] Similarly, blessed Job said, "My soul is wearied of this life."[274] And, reflecting the same

---

[273] Tobit 3:6.
[274] Job 10:1.

sentiment, Saint Paul wrote, "O wretched man! Who shall free me from this body of death?"[275]

The soul which has effectively cultivated the virtue of contemplation will be filled with a deep thirst for God, the font of life. This experience is reflected in the words of the psalmist: "Just as a deer thirsts for running streams, so does my soul desire You, O Lord."[276] In accordance with this, Saint Gregory writes, "The contemplative life is to retain love of God and one's neighbor with all one's thoughts, but to withdraw from exterior actions, and to rest in the desire of the Creator. The contemplative soul is inflamed with longing to see the face of Christ so that it comes to consider the affairs of practical life a burden which must be borne rather than a temptation. Instead, it will yearn to be present amongst the choirs of angels in heaven and to rejoice there in the eternal and imperishable delight of God's presence."

A sign of false or counterfeit contemplation is when a person claims to have received from God some message which is contrary to the truths of Sacred Scripture [or contrary to the teachings of the Church]. Because of such false contemplation, people will arrogantly and temerariously strive to defend such perverse opinions. Out of such erroneous beliefs resulting from non-genuine

---

[275] Romans 7:24.
[276] Psalms 41:2.

contemplation arose all the various heresies of the past—including the Arians, who denied the consubstantiality of the Son with the Father, and the Sabellians, who confounded the distinction of persons within the Trinity, asserting that these were differences in name only. [For all the members of the Trinity are consubstantial in respect to divinity, but] the Father alone is unbegotten, the Son alone is the only-begotten, and the Spirit is the one who proceeds from both.[277]

A PRAYER TO GOD FOR CONTEMPLATION

O Lord, the contemplation of You is the highest possible delight of the soul. For You reveal the wonders of Your being and the splendors of Your perfection to those who gaze upon You with eyes of awe and adoration. Grant me the grace to withdraw my thoughts and affections from all worldly distractions. Indeed, to those who contemplate You, all other things become a burden and a mere duty.

---

[277] This statement seems to be included here purely for the purpose of highlighting or explaining the errors of the Arians and Sabellians. Saint Albert was, of course, a teacher by profession and temperament, and seems to be taking the opportunity of reminding his readers of orthodox doctrine. On the other hand, he may be inserting this articulation of Trinitarian doctrine here to lead the reader to contemplation of this highest and most beautiful of all mysteries.

O Lord—
May I love You, and in loving You, desire You;
May I desire You, and in desiring You, seek You;
May I seek You, and in seeking You, find You;
May I find You, and in finding You, be forever
    united with You;
And in being united with You, may I share forever
    in Your eternal bliss. Amen.

34

DISCRETION

True discretion consists in the ability to discern prudently between the Creator and created things, and to recognize this distinction accurately and clearly in all situations. Similarly, it includes the ability to distinguish between what is good, what is better, and what is best; and what is bad, what is worse, and what is worst of all.

These principles of true discretion, if fully acquired, result in a wise appreciation and understanding of a great many more particular questions and matters, including:

- how much any good thing is to be desired, and how much any bad thing is to be avoided;
- how much reverence a person ought to give a superior, and how much clemency a superior should extend to his subordinates;
- how one ought to behave towards the dead, and how one ought to behave towards the living;

- how one should treat one's predecessors, and how one should treat one's successors;
- how one should treat friends so that they are loved *in* God;
- how one should treat enemies so that they are loved *because* of God;
- which things should be done privately, in the presence of God alone, and which things should be done publicly, in the sight of all;
- how the body is to be appropriately refreshed, and how the spirit is to be suitably nourished;
- the type of clothing one ought to wear;
- when one should eat and drink, and when one should abstain from eating and drinking;
- how much and what one should consume;
- when one should keep vigil and when one should sleep, and for how long;
- when one should pray or weep, and when work is to be done;
- how one should respond to praise or to correction and criticism;
- when one should speak, and when one should keep silence;
- how much one should speak, and with whom, and for what reasons, and when, and in which places;

- when and to what extent one should accept gifts, or retain them, and when and how much one should give to another.

To be able to judge wisely in all these matters indicates that the virtue of true discretion has been fully acquired.

Discretion may be described as the teacher and master of all other virtues, for it establishes them all in their proper order and degree. For example, where discretion is absent, the virtue of love lacks order, and cannot successfully determine who and what should be loved more and who and what should be loved to a lesser degree.

Indeed, Saint Augustine warns us of the necessity of maintaining proper order and degree in all our virtues, even humility. "Where excessive humility is displayed by a leader," he wisely observes, "then his authority will be undermined."

Similarly, obedience, if not regulated by discretion, may become blind and foolish if it goes so far as to follow wicked or impious commands. Without discretion, generosity can easily become improvidence and wastefulness. Indiscrete fear can become desperation, and indiscrete hope can be converted into presumption. Justice, if not tempered by discretion, can easily become severity and harshness. Patience, mercy, gentleness, and kindness, if not moderated and ordered by discretion, often give rise to the flourishing of evils and vices. For, indeed, patience, mercy, gentleness, and kindness, when excessive and improperly applied, can lead to the disintegration of religion, the falsification of the truth, the violation of chastity, and the undermining of constancy. Thus discretion is required for all the other virtues to work properly.

The virtue of discretion is often increased by the experience of a failure in one of the other virtues. A person may "slip" in some virtue in a great many ways. For example, he may fall:

- from humility into pride or vainglory;
- from charity into envy;
- from patience into anger;
- from gentleness into aggression;
- from fervor into tepidity;
- from chastity into fleshly lust;
- from love of poverty into avarice;
- from peace into discord;
- from obedience into rebellion;
- from gravity into flippancy;
- from piety into dissolution;
- from love of silence into loquaciousness or gossip;
- from spiritual love into carnal love;
- from hope into presumption;
- from holy fear into servility or timidity;

- from justice into severity;
- from mercy into softness and permissiveness;
- from constancy into capriciousness; and
- from truthfulness into dissimulation.

Whenever a person recognizes that he has undergone such a fall, it will often serve to make him more careful and circumspect in the future, and thus to strengthen the virtue of discretion.

True discretion may be effectively nurtured in a number of ways, including through devout and attentive reading of the Scriptures, reflecting upon the examples of the saints, and accepting frequent advice from wise persons. Concerning this last practice, Scripture counsels us, "Always seek advice from the wise."[278] Similarly, we read of the Lord saying to Saint Paul, "Arise and enter the city: and there you shall be told what you ought to do."[279] Likewise, Christ sent forth a leper, saying, "Go and show yourself to the priests."[280] [Both of these cases may be understood as an exhortation to seek counsel from the wise.] It is important to note that in the second case, Christ did not send the healed man to *one* priest only but directs him to "show himself to the *priests*." In this way, if one priest or advisor happens to be less discrete or wise, wisdom may be sought from another.

---

[278] Tobit 4:19.
[279] Acts 9:6.
[280] Luke 17:14.

SIGNS OF TRUE AND DEFICIENT DISCRETION

A sign of true discretion is when a person attempts to obtain the advice of the wise in undertaking all important matters in life. And when this is not practical or possible, he will deliberate carefully with his own conscience, in the presence of God. In these ways (either through the counsel of experienced persons or through careful and prayerful reflection), he shall fulfill what is written: "My child, do nothing without taking counsel, and then you shall not regret it."[281] But a person with true discretion will not trust entirely in his own conscience or judgment, unless it is confirmed by Scripture. Neither will he trust completely in his own interpretation of Scripture, unless it is confirmed by the tradition and magisterium of the Church.

Evidence of a lack of, or deficiency in, discretion is when a person endeavors to undertake fasts, vigils, prayers, penance, and tears that exceed his capacities. When this occurs, persons can end up ruining their own health and destroying their energy within a short space of time, and render themselves useless for long-term service of the Lord. But, alas, in our own times (so tepid and half-hearted are we) there are very few people who err through such excessive fervor!

---

[281] Ecclesiasticus 32:24.

Another (and contrary) sign of a lack of discretion is an excessive concern about the health and well-being of the body, which can reach a point that people refuse to go without any comfort and convenience. Such people may imagine themselves to be saying, "Lord, for your sake I am guarding my strength!"[282] But at the same time, they are often neglectful of their spiritual health and do not provide their souls with the nourishment they need. Indeed, a healthy spiritual life cannot be maintained without effort, discipline, and dedication. Hence it is that Saint Augustine wrote, "While we all fear physical illness, we can easily neglect the health of our souls." This is because the flesh, when it is indulged and pampered, actually debilitates the spirit. Again, Saint Augustine testifies, "As a worm devours wool or wood, and as fire burns up grass or straw, so the flesh, if overindulged and pampered, devours and burns up the spirit."

Such people do not realize that overindulgence and pampering of the flesh is harmful not only to the spirit but even debilitating to the flesh itself. Thus it is that people who constantly indulge themselves not only fail to serve God fervently and devoutly but also typically become physically weak and ill.[283]

---

[282] Psalms 58:10.

[283] This observation, which reflects very accurately the conditions of modern society, is no doubt based upon Saint Albert's own empirical ob-

A Prayer to God for Discretion

O God, eternal wisdom,
Protect me from all strife,
And grant me true discretion
With which to rule my life.

Help me discern most wisely
With measure and restraint;
Lord, purify my judgments
From folly's foolish taint.[284]

---

servations. Cardinal Giovanni Bona, writing in the seventeenth century, similarly remarked that "gluttony kills more people than the sword."
[284] This prayer has been rendered in verse for the sake of variety. It is a very free adaptation rather than a literal translation, but contains all the essential sentiments of the original.

35

SHARING JOY[285]

To share the joy of God means to rejoice in all the infinite blessedness and perfections of God, which pertain eternally to His very essence. These perfections and beatitudes of God include omnipotence, wisdom, goodness, et cetera. And they are so immeasurably great that nothing at all could be lacking from them. Such is their magnitude—or rather, infinitude—that they suffice not only to provide God with eternal bliss but also to fill all of creation with the golden radiance of His blessedness.

Another aspect of sharing the joy of God is taking delight in His creation and ordering of the heavens and the earth, and all that is in them, and admiring all of His works from the very beginning of time until the end of the age. The greatest of all these works of the Lord are His own incarnation, passion,

---

[285] The word used by Saint Albert here is '*congratulatio*' (literally, 'congratulation'). However, he indicates by this not merely an expression of joy at another's success or happiness, but a deeper sharing of the joy of others.

resurrection, and ascension, as well as His sending forth of the Holy Spirit, and His perfect judgment of all beings at the end of time, including humans, angels, and demons.

We may also share in the joy of God by being filled with wonder and happiness at the vast symphony of praise that is perpetually sung to Him, both by the angels and saints in heaven and by mortal human beings on earth.

Sharing the joy of our neighbors has several aspects. It includes:

- rejoicing with the holy dead in their enjoyment of the glories of heaven;
- rejoicing with repentant sinners in their conversion;
- rejoicing with the righteous in their virtue and goodness of life;
- rejoicing with the Church in the celebration of the sacraments and the gifts of the Holy Spirit; and
- rejoicing with all the saints, especially the Blessed Virgin Mary, the patriarchs, prophets and apostles, and all the elect in the spiritual gifts they have received from God, and accepted in God.

We should be led to the cultivation of the virtue of sharing joy by a consideration of its immense usefulness and the stupendous benefits it confers. By learning how to share joy (both the joy of God and of others), we participate in the glory and beatitude of God, the angels and the saints, and all the graces and virtues of the Church. By sharing in the joy of others, in a certain sense we make it our own joy.

We should also reflect that the sharing of joy between the persons of the Holy Trinity—the Father, the Son, and the Holy Spirit—was the source and origin of all creation. This mutual sharing of joy within the Trinity always was, is now, and ever shall be the originating font of all divine actions.

SIGNS OF VIRTUOUS AND FALSE JOY

A sign that a person has achieved a virtuous sharing in joy is that he delights in all the things that are truly of God. This includes all matters arranged and decreed by the Church, all the works and judgments of God, and the most holy examples of Our Lord Jesus Christ. This joy he will not only experience in his heart but communicate to others by means of his words and actions. The person with this virtue will share in the joy of all the spiritual and natural gifts of the angels and saints in heaven, and also will rejoice over all the blessings received by other human beings here on earth.

A sign of false or counterfeit sharing of joy is when a person expresses happiness in the works of God in heaven and on earth and the merits of the saints, yet shows clear disdain for these in his actions. Such persons are reproved by the Lord through the prophet Isaiah, who said, "This people glorifies me with their lips, but in their hearts they are far from me!"[286] Likewise, those who refuse to rejoice with the Church over its successes and blessings cut themselves off from its body.

A PRAYER TO SHARE THE JOY OF GOD AND OTHERS

May my soul rejoice—indeed, may it be overwhelmed with happiness!—to contemplate Your own marvelous beatitude and perfection, O Lord. May I take delight in the magnificent and beautiful harmony that You have established in Your creation, and the awe-inspiring and transcendent wisdom that permeates all Your judgments. Above all, may I never cease to exult at the wondrous works of Your grace in achieving our redemption! For Your blessedness is so infinite that it fills the entire universe with ineffable joy and jubilation.

Lord, teach me to rejoice in Your joy, to love Your works, to revere Your judgments, to feel gratitude for Your benefits (both to myself and my neighbor), and never to cease to extoll Your glory, for You live and reign forever and ever. Amen.

---

[286] Isaiah 29:13.

36

CONFIDENCE

True and perfect confidence consists in that tranquil security of mind that arises from the conviction that God never abandons those who love Him. This type of holy confidence is reflected in the words of Scripture: "No one hoping in the Lord has ever been confounded. And has there ever been anyone who followed His precepts, and was abandoned?"[287]

A person with this confidence will be certain that God is always present whenever he faces trials and tribulations, and, what is more, that He is ever-ready (at the appropriate time) to free him from his troubles and to bestow His glory upon him. This is in accordance with the verse of the psalm, in which the Lord promises, "When he is in trouble, I will rescue him, and I shall glorify him."[288]

Daniel exhibited this type of confidence when he was cast into the lion's den, as did Noah in his ark, and Joseph when

---

[287] Ecclesiasticus 2:11–12.
[288] Psalms 90:15.

he was thrown into a well by his brethren. The same invincible confidence was displayed by the three young men when placed in the burning furnace by King Nebuchadnezzar. And all of these were safely liberated from their predicaments and plights by the mighty and merciful hand of the Lord.

Hence it is that Saint Peter writes, "The Lord knows well how to rescue the just from tribulation."[289] Similarly, in the book of Tobit, Sarah says, "But this every one is sure of that worships You—that his life, if it be under trial, shall be crowned: and if it be under tribulation, it shall be delivered therefrom: and if it be under correction, it shall be allowed to come to Your mercy. For You are not delighted in our being lost, O Lord. After a storm, You bestow tranquility and calm, and after tears and weeping, You grant joy to the heart."[290]

A person blessed with the virtue of holy confidence will never doubt that his prayers and supplications are always heard by God. Saint John Chrysostom writes of this confidence, saying, "If you approach the Lord with this mindset, and say, 'I will not depart until my prayer has been answered,' then your prayer *will* be answered—assuming you ask for something which it befits God to bestow, and which it is appropriate for you to receive."

Complete confidence is a most praiseworthy virtue, and extremely meritorious in the sight of the Lord. The apostle

---

[289] 2 Peter 2:9.
[290] Tobit 3:21–22.

Saint Paul testifies to this when he says, "Do not lose your confidence, for it will earn for you a great reward."[291]

If we consider the immense generosity of God and the fact that He very often bestows upon us more than we dare to ask for, we will soon be led to this virtue of pious confidence. God the Father created us in the divine image of the Holy Trinity. God the Son conferred on us His own sacred body as food, and His own most precious blood as drink. He even gave up His very life as the price of our redemption! Who, indeed, could possibly ask for or imagine more stupendous evidence of God's generosity towards us?

The recollection of Christ on the cross ought to inspire us all to unwavering confidence. Concerning this, Saint Bernard wrote, "Who should not be filled with hope and confidence in the generosity and goodwill of the Lord towards him, if he considers the disposition of Christ upon the cross? For His sacred head was lowered, that He might offer us His kiss. His arms were extended so that He could embrace us all. His hands were pierced so that He could give more freely of His graces and blessings. And His side was opened by a lance so that His love might flow forth from His Sacred Heart without restraint or hindrance. His whole body was stretched out, as if He willed to give us Himself—and, in giving Himself, to give us everything!"

---

[291] Hebrews 10:35.

SIGNS OF TRUE AND DEFICIENT CONFIDENCE

A sign of true and sincere confidence is for a person not to be obsessively burdened by the reproaches of his own conscience, [but rather to have faith in the forgiveness of God]. This is in accordance with what is written by Saint John: "If our conscience does not condemn us, then we have faith in God, that whatever we ask of Him we shall receive."[292]

Another indication of true confidence is for a person to apply himself constantly and tirelessly to good works. This applies especially to the good works of spiritual almsgiving, which includes the forgiveness of hurts and offenses one sustains, and offering prayers for others.

A further sign of true holy confidence is when a person is fully convinced that his past sins (such as those committed in his youth) have been forgiven—provided, of course, he has repented of them and done appropriate penance.

Saint Augustine testifies that "if anyone, in the final throes of an illness and about to die, sincerely wishes to repent for his sins and does penance, then he shall be reconciled and will leave this world in a reconciled state. We do not deny that such a person will obtain what he seeks, but we cannot presume that anyone who repents upon his death bed will have a good departure. We cannot take it

---

[292] 1 John 3:21–22.

for granted—I won't deceive you—we cannot take it for granted! The faithful who have led good lives will leave this world safely. And those who pass away immediately after baptism will pass to the next world with perfect assurance. A person who repents and does penance while still in good health and then lives justly afterwards, will also certainly have a good end. But as for those who repent in their very last moments—I cannot claim to be sure about that."[293]

And a little later in the same sermon, Augustine continues:

> Have I said that a sinner repenting only at the last moment will be damned? No, I have not said this. But do I say that he will be liberated? Neither do I say this. What, then, do I say about him? I say honestly that I do not know. I do not presume anything, and I do not promise anything. Do you wish yourself to avoid this doubt? Then, repent now, before you have reached your final moment! Do you wish to escape facing dreadful uncertainty at the end of your life? Then, do penance now! For if you do penance now and refrain from sin, when your last day arrives, you shall be secure. Why will you be secure? Because you have already repented while you were still able to do fitting penance.

---

[293] See Augustine, *Sermon 393*. Augustine was writing here before sacramental reconciliation was a standard practice.

If, however, you repent of your sins on your deathbed or in the throes of your final illness, then you are repenting of sins you are no longer able to commit. It will not be you who has departed from your sins but rather it will be your sins which have departed from you. "But how shall I know," you say, "if God has forgiven me?" A very good question! How shall you know, indeed? I myself do not know. And I know only that I do *not* know.

The reason I would recommend repentance to a dying sinner is that I do not know whether or not it will be effective. It may be, or it may not be. If I knew for sure that it would not be effective, I would not recommend repentance. But if I knew for sure that deathbed repentance was effective and sufficient, I would not be warning and admonishing you as I do now. There are two possibilities: either something is known or it is not known. But which of these you will face, I do not know. Therefore, cling to what is certain, and strive to flee from everything which is uncertain!

The person who wishes to have full confidence in the efficacy of his repentance should apply his efforts to spiritual works, pursuant to the words of Isaiah: "Those who hope in the Lord shall renew their strength, and take to themselves the wings of an eagle! They will run, and not grow weary. They shall walk and not grow tired."[294] In this man-

---

[294] Isaiah 40:31.

ner, it often happens that those who formerly applied their strength and energies to the wicked works of the flesh come to apply such powers to the holy deeds of the spirit!

A sign of a lack of holy confidence is when a person doubts the efficacy of the grace of redemption, and prefers to wallow in his own iniquity. Hence it is written in the Gospel: "We know that God does not hear sinners, but if anyone is a true worshipper of God and does His will, then God will hear him."[295] And in the psalms, it is written: "If I had found wickedness in my heart, God would not have heard me."[296] And the prophet Isaiah likewise testifies, "Your iniquities separate you from God, and your sins cause His face to be concealed from you."[297]

A form of false or erroneous confidence is when a person believes that because of the mercy and clemency of God, both the good and the evil shall be saved on the Day of Judgment, since Christ died for the salvation of all.[298] In clear contradiction of this opinion is what the Lord Himself

---

[295] John 9:31.

[296] Psalms 65:18.

[297] Isaiah 59:2. The point which Albert is making in this paragraph is that sinfulness and lack of confidence in the efficacy of prayer and penance go hand in hand. Both give rise to each other, and feed each other.

[298] The belief in universal salvation (or "apocatastasis") has been a recurrent heresy in Christian thought. Albert's comment here is evidence that it enjoyed a certain currency in the thirteenth century.

says: "[The wicked] shall go forth to eternal punishment, but the righteous shall go to eternal life."[299]

Another form of false or presumptuous confidence is when a person believes that he can have all his sins forgiven and be restored to the grace of innocence whenever and however he pleases [without any real contrition or sorrow]. Yet another case of false or erroneous confidence is when a person assumes that because God has given him an abundance in the goods of this world, he shall also receive an abundance of eternal joys in the life to come. But this is clearly not necessarily the case at all, as is witnessed in the psalm: "Those who hope in the greatness of their riches shall be disappointed."[300]

A PRAYER TO GOD FOR HOLY CONFIDENCE

O Lord, it is a great wonder that each created entity was given the miraculous gift of existence itself, before they could possibly have desired it or done anything to deserve it! It is a no less awesome wonder that You impressed Your image and likeness upon human beings. For what could any person possibly do to merit such a distinction and honor? And who shall not be amazed that You gave Your beloved and only-begotten Son for us to wash away our sins with His precious blood and to unite our nature to Your divinity?

---

[299] Matthew 25:46.
[300] Psalms 51:9.

Who would not be filled with complete confidence in You if they bear in mind the fathomless generosity that You have exhibited in each case? Who would doubt Your love and mercy for even a moment if they but gaze upon the cross of Christ? Who would question Your kindness and tenderness when they behold the wound on His open side, from which poured forth the crimson dew of divine clemency in such copious torrents?

O God, You are my goodness and my hope! Vouchsafe unto me perfect faith and confidence in Your saving mercy. And, inspired by this confidence, let me diligently apply myself to contrition and penance so that I may leave this world free of all the entanglements of empty vanity and purified from every stain of sin. Amen.

37

DISDAIN FOR WORLDLY THINGS

Thue disdain for worldly matters[301] is to be ready to renounce all material possessions, social prestige and rank, and ecclesiastical distinctions for the sake of God. It means being able to withdraw oneself from all fleshly attachments and all secular customs for the sake of the hope of eternal beatitude. Saint John exhorts us to this detachment in his epistle, saying, "Do not love this passing world, nor anything in this world."[302]

Saint Augustine acquired this detachment from earthly things when he came to find that no earthly thing could bring him satisfaction or fulfillment. And similarly, Saints

---

[301] The Latin text here uses the expression *contemptus mundi*, meaning literally "contempt of the world." This was a standard expression and should not be understood as carrying the strong negative sense of the modern English word "contempt." For this reason, the terms "disdain" or "detachment" have been chosen, as conveying the intended sense more authentically.

[302] 1 John 2:15.

Agnes, Catherine, and Cecilia, and other holy virgin-martyrs disdained this world and all its adornments for the sake of their love for Our Lord Jesus Christ.

We should be induced to feel a certain disdain for worldly things when we consider the inconstancy and unreliability that they exhibit towards all those who pursue them. The inconstancy of this world was even experienced by its Creator Himself. For when our Lord arrived in Jerusalem on Palm Sunday, He was greeted with great applause and acclamation, as the crowds exclaimed, "Hosanna to the Son of David! Blessed is He who comes in the name of the Lord; Hosanna in the highest!"[303] But just a few days later, on the Friday of the same week, the same crowds cried out to Pilate, "Crucify Him! Crucify Him!"[304] and, "If He were not a criminal, we would not have handed Him over to you."[305] And when He was dying on the cross, these crowds mocked and derided Him saying, "If You are the Son of God, save Yourself!"[306] The same people who had applauded and venerated Him with palms and flowers now crowned His head with thorns, and struck Him with rods and whips. And the very same people who had cast their vestments on the ground before Him on Palm Sun-

---

[303] Matthew 21:9.
[304] John 19:6.
[305] John 18:30.
[306] Matthew 27:40.

day in adoration stripped Him of His garments in contempt on Good Friday. [Such, indeed, is the inconstancy of this passing world!]

A consideration of the grave perils that result from loving the things of this world ought to teach us to regard them with disdain. For the apostle James asks us, "Do you not realize that friendship with the world is enmity to God? For whoever wishes to be a friend of this world makes himself an enemy of God"[307] For the world hated the Lord Jesus, as He Himself testified to the apostles: "If the world hates you, know that it hated Me before you."[308]

Signs of True and False Disdain for Worldly Things

A sign of true disdain for the things of this world is when a person will not be swayed either by the temptation of material pleasures or deterred by threats, nor will he be influenced by any human praise or vituperation.

But a manifestation of false or insincere disdain for earthly things is when a person begins to renounce material pleasures only when poverty or old age compels him to do so. In such cases, he has not really left the world at all, but rather the world has left him. But—alas—how very many

[307] James 4:4.
[308] John 15:18.

people there are who renounce sin only when they find themselves no longer capable of sinning!

A PRAYER TO GOD FOR
DETACHMENT FROM THE WORLD

This world is but a passing shadow,
And filled with empty toys,
Its pains don't last forever,
And neither do its joys.

O Lord, let all my longings
Be fixed on things above.
Not on short-lived pleasures,
But everlasting love![309]

---

[309] This prayer has been rendered in verse for the sake of variety. It is a very free adaptation rather than a literal translation, but contains all the essential sentiments of the original.

38

MORTIFICATION OF THE FLESH

Genuine and fruitful mortification of the flesh occurs when a person willingly disciplines his own body by means of fasts, vigils, prayers, works of penance, and abstinence from delights in either food or drink. By means of such measures, the flesh is brought into obedience to the spirit. The apostle Paul did this when he said, "I treat my body hard and relegate it to servitude, lest perhaps when I preach to others, I myself may be found at fault."[310] And Judith, despite being a young, rich, and beautiful widow, is said to have fasted every day, with the exception of special feasts.

A consideration of the great usefulness and benefits of mortification of the flesh ought to encourage us to cultivate it diligently. For by the denial and disciplining of the flesh, the spirit is rendered stronger and more vigorous. Saint Paul testifies to this when he writes, "When I am weak (that is, in

---

[310] 1 Corinthians 9:27.

the flesh), then I am strong (in the spirit)."[311] And, conversely, overindulgence of the flesh vitiates the vigor of the spirit, as Saint Augustine observes: "Pampered flesh burns up and consumes the soul, just as a fire devours stubble."

Signs of True and Deficient Mortification of the Flesh

A sign of the healthy flourishing of this virtue of mortification is when a person supplies the flesh only with what is necessary, and indulges in nothing for the sake of pleasure or gratification alone.[312] This is in accordance with the words of the apostle, who writes, "We are not debtors to the flesh, that we should live according to the flesh."[313] For the impulses and cravings of pleasure demand a multitude of things and still can never be satisfied, but true necessity of sustaining our life and health demands but little, and what it does need is very simple.[314]

---

[311] 2 Corinthians 12:10.

[312] Albert is not here prohibiting occasional freer enjoyment of food or drink, especially if this is done out of courtesy or hospitality. The observance of feast days, with celebratory meals, was a regular part of life within religious communities in his time.

[313] Romans 8:12.

[314] This is a paraphrase of an oft-quoted proverb attributed to Epicurus: "The needs of nature are but few and simple, and easily satisfied, but the demands of pleasure and ambition are many, and can never be fulfilled."

Saint Paul, in the same epistle [to the Romans], goes on to warn us of the evils resulting from overindulgence and pampering the flesh. "If you live according to the flesh, you shall die. But if, for the sake of the spirit, you mortify the flesh, then you will surely live."[315] Elsewhere, he identifies also the multitude of the evil works which spring up from enslavement to the desires of the flesh, telling us that "the works of the flesh are manifest. They are adultery, fornication, impurity, immodesty, idolatry, sorcery, hatred, contentions, jealousies, outbursts of wrath, selfish ambitions, dissensions, heresies, envy, murders, drunkenness, gluttony, and the like. Of these I tell you now, just as I also told you in time past—those who practice such things will not inherit the kingdom of God."[316]

Another sign of true mortification is when a person (to use the words of Christ), "hates his soul in this world."[317] Saint Gregory explains that to "hate one's soul in this world" means to refuse to acquiesce to its lower or earthly impulses, to conquer its carnal appetites, and to do battle against the craving for pleasure. By overcoming these lower impulses, the soul is led to aspire to what is nobler and

---

[315] Romans 8:13.
[316] Galatians 5:19–21.
[317] John 12:25. Saint Gregory's interpretation shows that the expression "hate" should not be understood in the sense of a violent or adversarial antipathy but rather as an orientation towards the higher aspirations of the soul, rather than those which are lower.

purer; by disdaining what is lower, its learns to love that which is higher.

But the person who fails to restrain his soul from its lower desires throws himself headlong into the snares of the devil. We are gravely warned about this in the book of Ecclesiasticus, in which it is written, "If you yield your soul over to its concupiscence, you shall make yourself the source of rejoicing for your enemies."[318] And thus it was that Delilah was able to hand over Samson, that most strong warrior, into the hands of the Philistines to be mocked and derided.[319]

There are certain people who only restrain their stomach and mouth from the pleasures of food and drink, but they do not restrain their tongues from wicked speech and self-indulgent conversation. They do not deny their senses of sight or hearing or touch from the vain impulses of curiosity, nor do they withhold their minds from impious and depraved thoughts. Such people have not truly acquired the virtue of mortification and self-denial at all!

It does not suffice simply to restrain the mouth and stomach from indulgence, while each of the other senses are permitted to remain unchecked and unrestrained. Hence it is that Saint John Chrysostom wisely observes, "Those who abstain from food or drink but still perform acts of wickedness make themselves into imitators of the demons—for

---

[318] Ecclesiasticus 18:31.
[319] Judges 16.

the demons are not tempted by food or drink [or other cravings of the flesh], but nevertheless unceasingly seek after all that is evil."

A Prayer for Self-Denial

O Lord, God of immeasurable power and wisdom, in creating our human nature You chose to unite the spirit and the flesh in an indissoluble bond. Each of these—the spirit and the flesh—may be described as the "parents" of a human being. For it is the spirit which imparts life to the flesh, and the flesh that makes the activities of the soul possible. Nevertheless, the spirit is of higher dignity, since it alone possesses intelligence and wisdom. The spirit or soul is the master in the union, and the body is its servant.

Accordingly, grant me the grace to discipline my body so that it performs its work obediently and happily. Let me guard myself against all overindulgence and pampering of the flesh, lest it become disobedient and rebellious. May I respond to the demands of necessity and not to those of luxury and sensory gratification.

Lord, teach me to take up my own cross. Help me to realize that by means of small and daily mortifications of my fleshly desires I am able to partake in Your own salvific death, and thereby to merit a share in the eternal glory of Your resurrection. Amen.

39

CONTRITION

True contrition consists of a feeling of sincere sorrow for all of the sins one has committed. This sorrow of contrition is something that is taken up of one's own free will. To be virtuous contrition, this sorrow should be proportionate to the nature and seriousness of the sin. It should include the intention of confessing the sin, and undertaking appropriate satisfaction, penance, or reparation. The experience of such sincere contrition proceeds from the grace of God.

But sorrow that is purely the natural result of some consequence of a sin committed, or which is not driven by the grace of God, does not bring about any particular profit to the soul. Regarding the depth and intensity of the virtuous sorrow of true contrition, the prophet Jeremiah says, "O Lord, I make great weepings unto Thee!"[320] The Lord Himself gives us a precept concerning the salubrious pain

---

[320] Jeremiah 6:26.

of true contrition in the book of the prophet Joel, in which He says, "Let not your garments be torn, but rather let your hearts be broken."[321] A consideration of the manifold sufferings of Christ—the crown of thorns, the nails, the rods, the whips, the cross, and the spear—is potently efficacious in moving the heart to purifying tears and healthful pain.

Unfortunately, true contrition is a somewhat rare virtue. As Saint Gregory observes, "There are many people who renounce the world, and give away all they possess. Yet, though this is a meritorious thing in itself, very often such people do not feel any true contrition or compunction for their past sins. Nor is it to be believed that wherever there are tears and sighs present, there is necessarily true contrition as well. For many people weep simply because they fear hell, or because they have suffered some punishment because of their sins, or because they feel a purely natural and instinctive sense of shame or guilt.[322] But true contrition includes genuine sorrows over all sins committed, all good works omitted, and all received graces which have been ignored or neglected."

We should be inspired to feelings of true contrition by a consideration of the great spiritual loss that we incur

---

[321] Joel 2:13.

[322] Saint Gregory is not saying here that the fear of hell and a sense of guilt or shame over one's sins are not commendable things. Rather, he is pointing out that these do not, in themselves, constitute true contrition.

through our sins. For they can cause us to lose the presence of the Holy Spirit and His gifts, divine graces of all kinds, friendship with the Holy Trinity, and the company of the angelic court. Again, what is it that we *acquire* through sin? Eternal death, the disapproval of God the Father, and estrangement from God the Son! These indeed are much worse and more fearsome than the dreadful flames of hell themselves, as Saint John Chrysostom testifies.

The usefulness of contrition and the many benefits that spring from it ought to lead us to cultivate this virtue. For contrition is able to delete all stains from the soul, and thus to free it from eternal death. It restores for a person the blessing of the Father, friendship with the Son, familiarity with the Holy Spirit, and companionship with the hosts of angels. Genuine contrition of heart is so powerful that even a little of this true contrition is able to earn forgiveness for more sins than even the greatest amount of almsgiving done without real sorrow for one's sins. All of these benefits, carefully weighed in the scale of the heart, ought to drive us to cultivate the virtue of contrition very earnestly.

SIGNS OF TRUE AND FALSE CONTRITION

A sign of the presence of true contrition is when a person would prefer to undergo all the sufferings of purgatory than to commit a single sin against our most kind and loving God. A person infused with a true spirit of contrition would prefer to be drawn into the depths of the underworld rather than to be drawn into sin, or to sustain all the torments of martyrdom rather than to stray from his holy intentions. Such a person would willingly undergo all the afflictions of sickness or poverty for the sake of making adequate satisfaction for his offenses and omissions.

But an indication of false contrition is when a person weeps over his sins and yet afterwards commits the exact same acts again (even if the sorrow he felt was genuine). In Ecclesiasticus, we are warned against this tendency: "If a person is purified following contact with a dead body, and afterwards touches it again, of what use was his washing?"[323] Similarly, if a person repents of a sin, but has no firm resolve to refrain from it in the future, of what use or profit is his repentance? How can it be considered to be really sincere?

Saint Augustine cautions against permitting any sin to be repeated and thus to become a habit. "Out of a perverse will," he writes, "springs up concupiscence. And if this is not resisted, the actions driven by concupiscence become a habit. And once they have become a habit, they eventually turn into a compulsion and necessity."

---

[323] Ecclesiasticus 34:30.

A Prayer to God for Contrition

May my eyes become fountains of tears, O God, for I have offended Your majesty! May my heart be broken with sorrow, for I have dared to violate Your laws and decrees!

Lord, You are the beloved Spouse of my soul. To You I offer the cruel scourgings of Your only-begotten Son, Our Lord Jesus Christ; I offer to You the bloody crown of thorns He wore, the bitter nails which pierced His hands and feet, the grim cross upon which He sustained His agonies, and the dire lance which pierced His holy side. Through all the sacred wounds that Your Son accepted for my salvation, I implore that my own heart should be deeply wounded with true contrition for my sins.

Light the fire of repentance in my soul so that its purifying flames may render me clean and fit to ascend to Your presence as a pleasing burnt offering. Let tears of contrition wash away the stains of my sin so that I may be ready to depart this world with full confidence, secure in the hope of heavenly glory. Amen.

40

HONEST CONFESSION

A true confession is a sincere and unconcealed manifestation of one's sins made in the presence of a legitimately ordained priest. The Lord Himself indicated this when He instructed the leper who had been healed to "go and show yourself to the priests."[324] Similarly, we find a commendation of the practice of confession in the epistle of James, in which he writes, "Confess your sins to each other."[325]

For a confession to be really true and meritorious, it should be complete, pure, deeply considered, and faithful. It should be made without reservation, according to what is written in the book of Lamentations: "Pour out your heart like water before the Lord."[326] In this "pouring out," the aspect of completeness is represented. Confession should not be made like giving forth water just drop by drop, but

---

[324] Luke 17:14.
[325] James 5:16.
[326] Lamentations 2:19.

whatever the penitent can bring to mind, he should reveal completely and fully to the priest, in a free outpouring.

The quoted text also specifies that confession should be poured out *like water.* Here it is indicated that confession ought to be pure and made with the simplicity and clarity of water. Confession should never be made out of servile fear or external compulsion, but purely and simply for the love of God.

Next, the verse says, "Pour out *your heart.*" Here, the necessity of deep consideration is indicated. For effective confession does not pertain only to words said, or actions performed or omitted. Rather, it ought to include all impure thoughts and unwholesome emotions, wayward intentions, harmful desires, perverse judgments, and presumptuous suspicions. For, as Origen states, on the Day of Judgment, our secret thoughts will either accuse us or defend us. For our thoughts and feelings, even if they are accompanied by no words or actions, leave a lasting impression on our soul, like a seal which has been pressed into wax.

Finally, the line of Scripture being considered says, "Pour out your heart like water *before the Lord.*" The words "before the Lord" indicate that our confession should be made with complete faith. All our sins are to be considered in the context of mindfulness of God. And whenever we, in our limited capacities and limited self-awareness, are able to recognize one single sin or fault within ourselves, God, in

His all-seeing omniscience and infinite wisdom, is certainly aware of a thousand others!

We should be encouraged to cultivate the virtue of honest confession by a consideration of the certain remission of sins and purification of the soul that it brings about. As Saint John testifies, "If we confess our sins, there is One who is faithful and just, who shall forgive our sins and cleanse us from all iniquity."[327] Indeed, honest confession has such power that the Holy Trinity—Father, Son, and Holy Spirit—all hear it and respond to it. It is wisely said that even if God already knows all our sins, He still awaits our confession of them.

SIGNS OF AN HONEST AND INSINCERE CONFESSION

A sign of the virtue of true and honest confession is when a person does indeed "pour out his sins like water." After this "pouring out," there should remain nothing of the color of sin, as if it were milk being poured out. Nor should there remain anything of the flavor or texture of sin, as if it were oil that were being poured out. Nor should there remain anything of the odor of sin, as if it were wine or vinegar being poured out. Rather, like *water* being poured out, no trace at all should remain evident in the vessel.

---

[327] 1 John 1:9.

Another indication of an honest confession is when a person is able to specify his sins with precision and accuracy in regard to number, seriousness, and degree.

An indication of insincere or improperly motivated confession is when a person confesses only for the sake of appearing to be faithful to the practice, or when he wishes to seem holy to others, or because of fear of the shame of being obliged to exclude himself from the reception of Holy Communion.

A PRAYER FOR HONEST CONFESSION

O Lord, by true confession
We're freed from all our sin,
From every taint of evil,
The guilt that lies within.

My hidden thoughts and secrets
I'll pour like water clear,
Revealing all my failings
To Your forgiving ear.[328]

---

[328] This prayer has been rendered in verse for the sake of variety. It is a very free adaptation rather than a literal translation, but contains all the essential sentiments of the original.

41

PENANCE

True penance, in an exterior sense, consists of voluntarily abstaining from certain permitted and lawful things in order to obtain mercy for having done acts which are not permitted. Thus penitents and enclosed religious abstain from red meat and from the wearing of fine garments. They fast and keep vigils and silence, and renounce their own wills through obedience to superiors. All the things they give up are, in themselves, perfectly licit for human beings, yet they forgo them for the sake of meriting God's mercy and grace more abundantly. This is in accordance with the injunction of John the Baptist, who exhorted the people to "do penance, for the Kingdom of God is at hand."[329]

The very necessity of penance ought to lead us to cultivate and practice this virtue. For without it, salvation is impossible to obtain, in accordance with the statement of the Lord: "Unless you do penance, you will all perish."[330]

---

[329] Matthew 3:2.
[330] Luke 13:3.

And similarly, Saint Augustine writes, "Sins, whether small or great, will never remain unpunished." Hence the Lord enjoined David to do penance for his sins, after he had sinned by conducting a census of his people, giving him the choice of either enduring famine for seven years, or falling into the hands of his enemies for three months, or suffering plague for three days. And David chose the last option, placing himself and his people into the hands of the Lord to be subjected to the perils of the plague.[331] Through this narrative, the necessity of penance to atone for sins is figuratively signified. For sins can be punished either by the eternal fires of hell (which is what is signified by the seven years of famine), or in purgatory (which is signified by the violent attacks of the enemy, lasting for three months), or by doing penance in this present life (which is signified by the three days of pestilence). It is certainly most advisable for us all to choose the last option, of penance in this life, since it involves the lightest suffering and passes by the most swiftly.

SIGNS OF TRUE AND FALSE PENANCE

A sign of true penitence is for a person to undertake works that amount to an adequate and fully commensurate atonement for his faults. The works of penance should

---

[331] See 2 Samuel 24:1–17.

be in accordance with the quantity and seriousness of the sins committed. The bitterness of the penance should be commensurate to the pleasures of the sins, the duration of the penance should be commensurate with the duration of the sins, and the multiplicity of the penance should be commensurate with the multiplicity of the sins. It is in accordance with this principle that John the Baptist urged, "Bring forth fruits of penance [which are] fitting [to the faults being atoned for]."[332]

Each illness of the body has its own suitable and necessary medicine, and there is no one single medicine or treatment that can cure every ailment of the body. In the same manner, each kind of sin and vice has its own particular kind of fitting and effective penance, [and unsuitable forms of penance are less efficacious as remedies. For example,] pride is not normally cured by almsgiving, nor is avarice corrected by fasting, nor are lustful thoughts removed by keeping vigils. But pride *is* corrected by works of humility, avarice is corrected by giving alms, lustfulness is remedied by physical austerity. Gluttony is effectively treated by practicing fasting, talkativeness is controlled by silent prayer, and envy is healed by fraternal charity. A suitable penance for theft must obviously include the restoration of whatever was stolen.

---

[332] Matthew 3:8 and Luke 3:8.

But even if a person is not capable of completing a penance that is fully commensurate with his sins, then (as Saint John Chrysostom says) the good Lord Himself will supply what is lacking. Thus if a person had acquired something unjustly and it is no longer possible to restore it to its rightful owner, fasting could suffice as atonement. But if the person was not able to fast for some reason, prayer would be sufficient. And if the person was not even able to pray (because of sickness of body or infirmity of mind), a good intention alone could be enough in the sight of God.

Pope Innocent [III] identified several indications of false or insincere penance. These include when the person undertaking the penance does not withdraw himself from the occasions of sin, or if he feels resentment or bitterness in his heart about the penance he is doing, or if he does not undertake to make suitable reparation for the injuries he has caused, or if he refuses to forgive others for injuries he himself has sustained.

Another sign of a false penance is when, after completing the prescribed work of atonement for a sin, the person then proceeds immediately to commit the same sin once again.

A Prayer to God for True Penance

O Lord, You are the most perfectly just and equitable Judge. You allow no merit or work of virtue to go unrewarded, and You permit no sin to remain unpunished. Yet, in Your immense mercy, You afford to sinners the opportunity to atone for their offenses by means of penance during this present life, and thus to avoid the dreadful torments of purgatory or the eternal flames of hell in the life to come.

Help me to bring forth worthy fruits of penance so that I may make satisfactory atonement for all my sins while I am still alive in this world. Through acts of penance, may I fulfill all that Your perfect justice requires of me, in accordance with my own limited strength and capacities. Merciful Lord, grant me the grace and wisdom to deny myself some of those things that are permitted to me in order to atone for my sinful indulgence in those things which are forbidden. Amen.

42

PERSEVERANCE

True perseverance comprises the frequent application of oneself to good works, continual efforts to attain to spiritual and moral perfection, and the most diligent observance of all graces and virtues until the moment of death. The Lord invites us to cultivate and embrace this virtue of perseverance when He says in the book of Revelation, "Be faithful unto death, and I shall bestow upon you the crown of life!"[333] Holy Job exhibited this virtue of perseverance in an exemplary degree when he declared, "Until I die, I shall not waver from my innocence."[334] Tobit also displayed this holy perseverance when he continued to bury the bodies of the dead, even though the king of Assyria had threatened to despoil him of his possessions and kill him because of this.[335]

---

[333] Revelation 2:10.
[334] Job 27:5.
[335] See Tobit 1:18–22.

A consideration of the great usefulness and benefits of holy perseverance ought to induce us to love and cultivate this virtue. For it is only by dint of perseverance that all our good works and all our other virtues can come to be consummated and crowned. Indeed, without perseverance, salvation is impossible, according to the words of Our Lord Jesus Christ Himself. For He declared, "It is the one who perseveres until the end who will be saved."[336] Without perseverance, no good work or virtue will be able to endure long enough to merit its reward. Without perseverance, nothing will be brought to completion or perfection!

For example, what did it profit the apostle and traitor Judas that he had once chosen to leave the world and to follow Christ? What benefit did his long-lasting friendship with Jesus bring him? Or the holy preaching, which he had so often listened to from the Lord's own mouth, or the multitude of miracles which he had so frequently witnessed, or the holy company of the other apostles with whom he had long been associated, or even the ministry of preaching and miracles which he himself had undertaken? For this traitor, Judas, had certainly been amongst the chosen twelve when the Lord said to them, "Go forth, and proclaim that the kingdom of God is at hand. Cure the sick, raise up the dead, cleanse the lepers, and cast out demons!"[337] [Clearly,

---

[336] Matthew 10:22.

[337] Matthew 10:7–8.

in the end, such good works did *not* assist Judas at all, since he lacked the virtue of holy perseverance to continue in the good path he had begun.]

SIGNS OF TRUE AND FALSE PERSEVERANCE

A sure sign of true perseverance is when a person will not deliberately depart from what he knows to be right in the face of any adversity, trial, or temptation—neither love of life, nor fear of death, nor threats, nor promises will be able to deter him from his holy resolve. This perseverance was exhibited by Susanna when she boldly declared, "If I have sinned, then let me die!"[338] Likewise, in the first book of the Maccabees, the brave Mattathias said, "Even if all the nations obey King Antiochus, and even if each one departs from the laws of their forefathers to submit to his wicked decrees, I and my sons and my brothers shall all remain unswervingly faithful to the law of our ancestors. May the Lord be merciful to us!"[339]

A sign of false or deluded perseverance is when a person has so much confidence in his own sanctity that he believes it is not possible for him to fall away. Out of this presumptuous confidence, a harmful and dangerous liberty of soul is born, and the person soon ceases to keep custody of his

---

[338] Daniel 13:22.
[339] 1 Maccabees 2:19–21.

own thoughts and actions. Hence it is impossible that such a person will be able to persevere in sanctity in the longer term. Indeed, if the holy apostles continued to live in this world of temptations and trials and they failed to keep custody of their minds and hearts, even they would eventually slip into sin! King David provides us with an instructive example of the importance of guarding oneself in order to achieve holy perseverance. For, although he was both wise and holy, he committed adultery and murder, all because he had neglected to keep custody of his eyes![340]

Prayer for Perseverance

O Jesus, make me constant
And faithful to Your law,
And teach me perseverance,
To stand firm evermore.

And let my heart not waver,
Nor wander from Your light;
Grant holy perseverance
In all that's just and right.[341]

---

[340] See 2 Samuel 11.

[341] This prayer has been rendered in verse for the sake of variety. It is a very free adaptation rather than a literal translation, but contains all the essential sentiments of the original.

SAINT ALBERT'S EPILOGUE

Omost holy Lord, I honestly confess to You, by the power of all the tears and the drops of blood-like sweat of Your beloved Son, that I myself (who have written this treatise) have not even arrived at the beginnings of a single one of the virtues! And I have certainly not attained to any of the lofty perfections that are described in this little treatise.

I rejoice, nevertheless, that [when we arrive in the kingdom of heaven] we shall possess each and every virtue in a manner surpassing anything the human mind may currently imagine. And I am sure that whoever possesses in perfection the virtues described in this book will be blessed in this life, and even more blessed in the life to come. Nevertheless, it is not to be imagined that it is necessary to achieve complete perfection in all the virtues (or even any one of the virtues) to attain salvation.

O Lord—filled with love for Your Son and the Holy Spirit, and admiring all Your creation—I humbly ask of You discretion and wise judgment. By means of this wisdom, may I learn to distinguish between those virtues which are merely the result of nature and those that are the holy fruit of Your grace.

Lord, I ask that You confer at least one perfect and true virtue on each person who reads this treatise, or hears it being read, or who reflects upon its contents. For I am certain that if anyone reaches perfection in just a single one of these virtues, they shall achieve perfection in them all. And whoever increases in one virtue will simultaneously grow in every other virtue too. But, conversely, whoever abandons just one virtue will begin to lose them all as well. And whoever lacks a single one of these virtues, will, in fact, possess no virtue at all—for all of the virtues are Your holy gifts, O Lord, and they are all mystically united in Your divine grace. Amen.